OM HEAD TO TOE

EDITORS

ARTHUR WIEBE
Project Director
Fresno Pacific College

LARRY ECKLUND
Project Director
Fresno Pacific College

SHERYL MERCIER
Elementary School Teacher
Lemoore Union Elementary School District
Lemoore, California

WRITING TEAM

ART AKERS
7–8 Science Teacher
Lodi Unified School District
Lodi, California

LOIS DUEPREE
6–8 Science Teacher
Fresno Unified School District
Fresno, California

JIM GRECO
7–8 Mathematics Teacher, GATE Program
Merced City School District
Merced, California

STEVE OWEN
6–8 Resource Teacher
Merced City School District
Merced, California

ANN PASLEY
5th Grade Teacher
Wasco Union Elementary School District
Wasco, California

GEORGE ROGERS
6th Grade Teacher
Modesto City School District
Modesto, California

YOLANDA ROJAS
5th Grade Teacher
Madera Unified School District
Madera, California

Illustrations by
Sheryl Mercier

i

AIMS (Activities Integrating Mathematics and Science) began in 1981 with a grant from the National Science Foundation. The non-profit AIMS Education Foundation publishes hands-on instructional materials (books and the monthly AIMS Newsletter) that integrate curricular disciplines such as mathematics, science, language arts, and social studies. The Foundation sponsors a national program of professional development through which educators may gain both an understanding of the AIMS philosophy and expertise in teaching by integrated, hands-on methods.

ISBN 1-881431-02-9

Printed in the United States of America

TABLE OF CONTENTS

	Student's Manual	Teacher's Manual

INDEX TO SKILLS

I HEAR, AND I FORGET
I SEE, AND I REMEMBER
I DO, AND I UNDERSTAND

-Chinese Proverb

INTRODUCTION

The selections "Are You Mean (x)," "Corpus Allaroundus," and "Dem Bones" are intended to be used as a unit. The basic information in the first activity is used to provide an information bank for the next activities. The diagram developed in the selection "Corpus Allaroundus" is utilized as the base for "Dem Bones." The outline can also be used in the development of all of the other portions of the human body. The drawings and diagrams can be made proportional and fitted into the appropriate place. Activities listed in the extensions can be utilized as independent or group research.

What is the Average Student Like?

I. **Topic Area**

The Average Student

II. **Introductory Statement**

The learner will utilize the information gathered from the measurement of his/her body to construct a personal chart and provide data for the development of class graphs.

III. **Math Skills**
   a. Graphing
   b. Charting
   c. Computing percent
   d. Measuring in metric units
   e. Measuring in conventional units
   f. Averaging
   g. Estimating

Science Processes
   a. Collecting data
   b. Analyzing data

IV. **Materials**

Tape measure (metric and conventional)
Pencil
Student worksheets, pages 1-8

V. **Key Question**

"What is the relationship between the individual and class norms?"

VI. **Background Information**

This is an introduction to metric measurement and the proportion of the human body. It is also an effective technique to introduce the students to an anatomy study. The students will also participate in a graph development process. Each student may be given a body part to graph and build a graph for that body part. The student should discover that there is a relationship between the individual and the group (bell curve).

VIII. **Procedure**
   1. Each student will estimate his/her measurement in metric units.
   2. The students will pair up and, using a metric tape, measure each other's bodies and record the measurements.
   3. Construct graphs, using the attached form (page 4), for each area on the form (eye color, hair color, weight, height). The graphs may represent all students, only boys, only girls, or only certain ages. Bar, composite, solid-line, or broken-line graphs may be constructed for comparison of different groups.

X. **Discussion**
   1. Can you find proportional relationships between body parts?
   2. Can you find any patterns in statistics (boys, girls, age, etc.)?

XI. **Extension**
   1. Develop graphs utilizing different characteristics.
   2. Develop graphs utilizing different groups or clusters.
   3. Develop graphs utilizing differences between estimates and actual measurements.
   4. Develop statistical analyses of relationships between height and various body parts.

CORPUS All AROUND US

I. Topic Area
Human Body Perimeter

II. Introductory Statement
This exercise introduces the student to the basic perimeter of his/her body.

III. Math Skills
a. Using ratio
b. Charting

Science Processes
a. Observing
b. Measuring
c. Predicting and estimating
d. Recording data
e. Generalizing

IV. Materials
One roll of white butcher paper
Six rolls of masking tape
Scissors
Paper clips (two per student)
Pencils and erasers
Black felt-tip pen for each student
Student worksheets, pages 9-10

V. Key Question
"What does my body 'outline' look like?"

VII. Management Suggestions
1. Teacher will cut sheet for each student.
2. Paper should be rolled, not folded, and paper clipped on ends.
3. Edges of paper should be taped with masking tape all around, both front and back.
4. Pencil should be held perpendicular to paper at all times during outlining procedure.
5. The original outlining should be given as homework, since the most accurate body outline requires a minimum of clothing.
6. Penciled outline should be clean, firm lines before finalizing it with black felt tip pen.

VIII. Procedure

Day One
1. Each student estimates own height and adds one meter to it.
2. Teacher measures and cuts paper according to this estimate.
3. Student tapes with masking tape the edges of his/her paper.
4. Student rolls and paper clips his/her sheet.
5. Student immediately puts name on outside of roll to help identify it at end of day.
6. Student takes roll home.

Homework
1. Unroll paper on clean, hard, flat surface and tape it down.
2. Student lies on back, centered on paper by family helper, arms extended at a minimum of 15 degrees, maximum of 45 degrees from body. Backs of hands are placed flat on the floor, fingers spread. Legs should be slightly spread and right foot turned so that outer edge is flat on paper. Head should be turned to the right.
3. Family helper proceeds with outlining the body, remembering to keep pencil perpendicular to paper surface at all times.

Day Two
1. Roll is returned to class.
2. Teacher examines each outline.
3. Students make final, firm-penciled outline.
4. Teacher distributes black felt-tipped pens.
5. Students carefully trace over the finalized outline.
6. Student originates a title to be put at the center. Student also pens name, class and date at bottom right.

Day Three
Using his/her own body outline, student measures with metric units and records the listed dimensions on student worksheet page 9.

X. Discussion
List and discuss the ratios and porportions of the listed body parts.

XI. Extension
1. Develop chart(s) from list of body parts ratios/proportions.
2. Measure your standing height and compare it to length of body outline. What factors might affect differences?
3. Determine the average of girls' heights and average of boys' heights. Is there a difference? Why?
4. Compare your measurements to the "Golden Proportion." See below* and student worksheet, page 8.

*"The Golden Proportion" The Anatomist is able to compute the stature of the individual by a formula based on the length of the thigh bone. Statistics show that the height of a man will be 1.88 times the length of this bone, plus 813.06 millimeters. In the female the figure is the length times 1.945 plus 728.44 millimeters. This formula may be applied to any human from the time of the ice age down. From *Our Human Body*, ©1962, Wilton Krogman.

"DEM BONES"
SKELETON

THE FRAMEWORK OF THE BODY

I. Topic Area
The Skeletal System

II. Introductory Statement
This activity will enable the students to visualize what the average skeletal system looks like.

III. Math Skills

Math Skills
a. Using ratio/porportion
b. Charting
c. Graphing
d. Averaging
e. Measuring

Science Processes
a. Observing
b. Measuring
c. Predicting and estimating
d. Recording data
e. Applying and generalizing

IV. Materials
Metric tape measures
Metric ruler
Meter stick
Butcher paper (lots)
Colored pencils—red, yellow, brown
Felt-tip pens, both fine and wide
Scissors
Pencils and large erasers
Student worsheets, pages 11-20

V. Key Question
"What does your skeletal system look like?"

VII. Management Suggestions
1. Be sure that your students know how to label as on worksheet page 13.
2. Stress that the initial sketch should be done lightly, as some corrections will be necessary. Perhaps use No. 4 pencils.
3. Be particularly careful about pairing students to avoid possible problems—girls with girls...

VIII. Procedure

Days 1-2
Follow procedure in Corpus Allaroundus, page 34, or use outlines students made during that activity. Outlining can be done at school if you pair girls with girls and boys with boys.

Day 3
1. Have students review the framework and bone structure of the human body, student worksheets pages 13-20.
2. If desired, take measurements required on student worksheets pages 11-12.
3. Referring to pages 13-20 and measurements taken in step 2, lightly sketch in the bone structure. (Note: pay particular attention to male and female pelvic differences, student worksheet page 20.)
4. Check each student's work for approximate accuracy.
5. Have students label the bones. Review with students proper labeling techniques: neatness, straightness and accuracy.
6. Finalize drawings.

X. Extensions
1. Extend drawings to include flexions, ligaments, tendons and joints.
2. Seek Golden Ratio.
3. Prepare reports on bone groups, etc.

SIDE VIEW OF SKULL

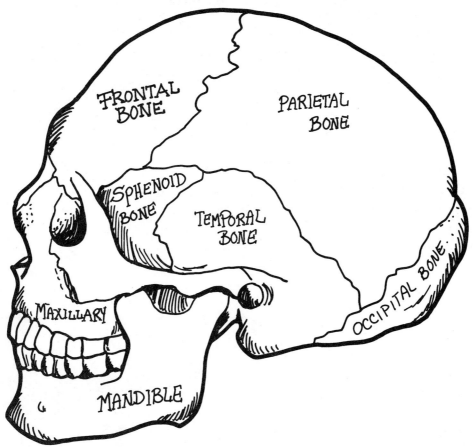

I. **Cranium** (skull)

Materials: two rulers and 8'-10' string.

Procedure: (1) Tie string to one end of the ruler—allow string to hang freely. (2) Place ruler #1 on top of head and allow string to hang downward until it touches nose. Use ruler #2 to measure from string to back of head. (3) Measure from base of ear lobe to top of head. (4) Measure from base of mandible (lower jaw) to top of head. This will give you enough measurements that when used in conjunction with mimeograph sheet should allow students to draw their own cranium.

II. **Humerus**

Measure from top of upper arm on outside of shoulder to bend of elbow. Starting point may be found by placing fingers on top of shoulder and slowly raising the arm. You should be able to feel terminal end of humerus rotate.

III. **Radius-Ulna**

Measure from bend of elbow to bend of wrist.

IV. **Phalanges** (fingers, toes)

Each joint can be measured at the joint crease.

V. **Carpals** (wrist)

Measure from terminal end of radius-ulna to base of palm (metacarpals); base of thumb to heel of hand (fleshy part of palm). Remember there are eight (8) bones which make up the carpals (wrist).

VI. **Metacarpals** (palm)

Measure from knuckle to an imaginary line at base of third joint of thumb and to fleshy part of palm at base of little finger.

VII. **Femur**

Measure from point where hip bends when leg is swung away from body to where leg bends at knee. Width at knee may be measured by placing two flat pieces of wood on each side of knee and measuring distance between (be careful to keep wooden pieces straight up and down).

VIII. **Patella** (kneecap)

Measurement accomplished by laying ruler on patella and measuring in two or three directions and drawing an enclosed arc between measurements.

IX. **Tibia-Fibula**

Measure from base of bended knee to bend in ankle. Upper width equals base of femur and forms an opposite-formed bone joint.

 From Head to Toe

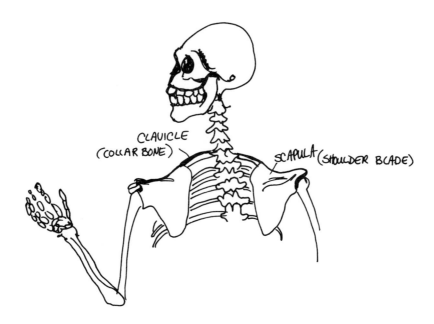

CLAVICLE (COLLAR BONE)

SCAPULA (SHOULDER BLADE)

X. **Metatarsals** (foot)

Measure from base of phalanges (toes) to bend in ankle.

XI. **Tarsals** (ankle)

Measure from heel to area where ankle bends. These bones fit between terminal ends of tibia-fibula which forms what is commonly called shin bones.

XII. **Pelvis**

Measure width from hip bone to hip bone. Base of pelvis is one half upper width. Gap between hip bones where spine connects to ilium-coccyx (backbone) is one-fourth upper width. Base of pelvis is one-fourth of lower width.

XIII. **Spine**

Cervical vertebrae are measured from base of skull to shoulders; remainder from shoulders to where you bend at the waist. Measure from dorsal (back) side rather than the ventral side.

XIV. **Clavical** (collar bone)

Measure from terminal end of shoulder to sternum (breast bone).

XV. **Scapula** (shoulder blade)

Using hand, place thumb on upper edge of shoulder blade and spread fingers until you are able to reach lower portion. Measure distance between spread. Width is determined by same method only from top of shoulder blade to base (see insert).

From Head to Toe

ARM YOURSELF

I. Topic Area

Muscle Strength (Arms and Shoulders)

II. Introductory Statement

Students will be able to compare the muscle strength of their arms and shoulders to that of their peers, within the same age and sex.

III. Math Skills

a. Averaging
b. Formulating

Science Processes

a. Classifying
b. Recording data
c. Analyzing and generalizing

IV. Materials

Pencils and paper
Chairs
Partner for recording
Student worksheets, pages 21-23

V. Key Questions

"How strong are you? How do you compare with others your own age?"

VI. Background Information

Chair push-ups are done in the following manner:
1. Student places chair against wall.
2. Student stands facing the chart and places hands on front edge of the chair.
3. Student places feet back so body is at 45° angle to the ground.
4. Arms straight and perpendicular to the body, back should be straight.

5. Student lowers himself/herself with his/her arms to the seat of the chair and returns to the original position.

VII. Management Suggestions

1. Give each student a number.
2. Classify each student by age and sex.
3. Pick a group leader for each category.
4. Put tables for age group on blackboard.

VIII. Procedure

1. Have each student do as many "chair push-ups" as possible (continuous movement, no resting between push-ups).
2. Have students record the number of push-ups completed on student worksheet page 21.
3. Give findings to group leader.
4. The leader will record the score on the blackboard under the right category.
5. Students will have worksheets identical to tables on the board.
6. Students should find the average for their age and group.

X. Discussion

1. How does the average of each group compare to the other averages in your class?
2. Does age make a difference in the amount of push-ups one can do?
3. How do you compare to the state norms? (student worksheet page 22)

XI. Extension

Have the classroom make a chart for their own norms. See student worksheets pages 22 and 23.

'YA GOTTA' HAVE HEART!

I. Topic Area
Heart Structure

II. Introductory Statement
All students will be able to demonstrate their knowledge of the heart structures by creating a heart model (exterior and interior).

Grabber Number One — Tennis ball squeeze
1. Try to do a heart's work with your hand.
2. Test the ease with which you can squeeze and get a grasp on the power of this mighty muscle. The force needed to squeeze a tennis ball is similar to the force needed to squeeze blood out of the heart.
3. Give it a good squeeze. If you squeeze seventy times a minute (the normal pulse), you will get a first-hand idea of how hard your heart works.

Grabber Number Two — Create your own stethoscope
1. Cut the top off of a plastic bottle.
2. Place a rubber tubing (obtained at any pet store or hardware store) on the top of your bottle top. Presto — stethoscope (see student worksheet page 25).

III. Science Processes
  a. Observing
  b. Predicting and estimating

IV. Materials
Pink clay
Blue clay
Balance
Diagram of the heart (student worksheet page 24)
Student worksheet page 25

V. Key Question
"What does the human heart look like?"

VII. Management Suggestions
Weigh out each lump of clay to each group. They must return the same weight at the end of class. (This will avoid clay flying through other rooms after class is out.)

VIII. Procedure
Divide the class into groups of two. One half of the groups will create the exterior of the heart. The other group will create the interior of the heart. Utilize blue and red clay in appropriate places. Refer to standard reference volumes for pictures of the heart.

X. Discussion
Why is one-half of the inside of the heart blue? (Lack of oxygen)

HOW DOES YOUR HEART RATE?

I. **Topic Area**

Pulse Rate

II. **Introductory Statement**

Students will gather information concerning their pulse rates.

III. **Math Skills**

a. Measuring
b. Estimating
c. Averaging
d. Graphing
e. Charting

Science Processes

a. Record keeping
b. Interpreting data
c. Observing

IV. **Materials**

Stop watch
Graph paper
Student worksheets, pages 26-33
Pencils

V. **Key Question**

"What is the effect of exercise on your pulse rate?"

VI. **Background Information**

The pulse is a measure of heartbeat. Each throb of the pulse represents one beat of the heart. The heart pumps blood through your circulatory system of arteries, capillaries, and veins. The total number of throbs in exactly one minute (60 seconds) is the pulse rate.

VII. **Management Suggestions**

This activity can be done in pairs, with one student recording and the other student taking his own pulse count. It can also be done on an individual basis at the teacher's discretion.

VIII. **Procedure**

Part One

1. Students may work singly or in pairs. Designate one as a recorder and one as the participant. The students may reverse roles and do the activity again (optional).
2. Give each student a copy of the worksheet. Have them sit quietly for at least three minutes while you pass out the worksheets.
3. Have the students count their pulse for ten seconds as their partner watches the clock. The teacher can use a stop watch if there is not a second hand on the clock. Use fingers rather than thumb for counting.
4. Have the students compute the pulse rate for one minute (see table 1).

Part Two

1. Have the students exercise for about one minute without stopping; running in place, deep knee bends, jumping up and down on one foot, walking in place, running in place, jumping jacks, or chair steps.
2. Have the students sit down immediately and count their pulse each minute for ten minutes as their partner keeps them informed of time. The recorder will complete table 2 on the student worksheet.
3. Have the students complete the graph and plot the points that represent their pulse rate for each minute after the exercise (see worksheet page 30).

X. **Discussion**

1. What are the effects of exercise on your pulse rate?
2. How many minutes passed before your pulse rate returned to your average pulse rate on table 2?
3. Why did your pulse rate increase when you exercised?

The Pressure's On

I. Topic Area
How Exercise Affects Blood Pressure

II. Introductory Statement
The learner will analyze the information gathered from the sample population to determine if activity in moderate amounts affects the blood pressure.

III.

Math Skills
a. Graphing
b. Charting
c. Computing percent
d. Averaging

Science Processes
a. Measuring
b. Record keeping
c. Interpreting data
d. Observing
e. Controlling variables

IV. Materials
One chart per student
A large chart for the class or an overhead
Two blood pressure kits (sphygmomanometer and stethoscope)
400 m measured course—track, playgound, etc.
Three colored markers and pencils
Student worksheets, pages 34-36

V. Key Question
"How does exercise affect blood pressure?"

VI. Background Information
The pressure from the arterial vessels is modified by two factors: the force of the heart and the change in size of the smaller vessels, the arterioles. Influences lessening the force of cardiac systole decrease the pressure, other things being equal. Hence, the pressure is less in sitting than in standing, less in lying than in standing, less in sleeping than in conscious states. Weakness of the heart muscle is reflected in a rise in pressure which during severe activity may reach 200 mm Hg. The distolic does not rise proportionally high, but it, too, rises.

VII. Management Suggestions
1. The time allotment is one period.
2. Randomly select ten students to participate in exercise in an experimental group.

VIII. Procedure
1. The students in both the control and experimental groups will have their blood pressure taken twice, once before and once after exercise.
2. The experimental group (10) will jog a 400 m lap, two students at a time. Record blood pressure as they come back.
3. The control group (20) will sit in the classroom and take and record blood pressure thirty minutes from activity.
4. Record information on the chart.

X. Discussion
1. Could you feel a physical change as you ran the lap?
2. Can you relate some of the physical changes to the increase in blood pressure? (flushed, heat, throbbing)
3. Is there a relationship between exercise and blood pressure? (Yes, there is even a variation between sitting, lying, standing, etc.)

XI. Extension
1. Have students lie down and have pressure taken, then standing, and then sitting.
2. Compare individual and group responses.
3. Average and graph for group, individual compared to group, etc.
4. Do the same for pulse rate, temperature, and respiration rate.

Step In Time

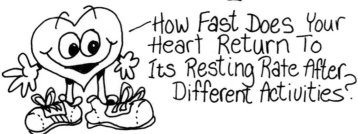

How Fast Does Your Heart Return To Its Resting Rate After Different Activities?

I. Topic Area
Pulse Rate

II. Introductory Statement
Students will gather information concerning their resting, sitting, standing, walking and running pulse rates. They will measure the time it takes their heart rate to return to the resting rate after engaging in physical activities.

III. Math Skills
a. Graphing
b. Averaging
c. Measuring
d. Charting

Science Processes
a. Observing
b. Measuring
c. Interpreting data

IV. Materials
Chair
Stop watch
Graph paper
Student worksheets, pages 37-38

V. Key Question
"How fast does your heart return to its resting rate after exercise?"

VIII. Procedure
1. Have students lie flat for two minutes, then check pulse rate, using fingers rather than thumb, and record data.

2. Have students sit quietly in a chair for two minutes, then check pulse rate and record data (resting data).
3. Have students sit in a chair for two minutes, then stand and check pulse rate, sit down and continue checking until pulse rate returns to normal. Record time and data.
4. Students walk in place for two minutes and record pulse rate. Sit down and check pulse rate until it returns to normal sitting rate. Then record time.
5. Students run in place for one minute. Record pulse rate and time required to return to normal sitting rate.
6. Run/sprint 50 yards. Record pulse rate and time needed to return to normal sitting pulse rate.
7. Chart each activity against resting data and develop composite graph of all information.

XI. Extension
1. Check dancers, swimmers, football players and basketball players to see which group has the shortest recovery period.
2. What was the lowest pulse rate recorded?
3. Do boys have a lower pulse rate than girls?
4. Does age of test group have any significance?
5. Who had the shortest recovery time? The longest? Why?
6. Students should run each phase of this experiment at least three times and record. They should also find the average for each experiment.

From Head to Toe

Temperature's Rising!

I. Topic Area
How Exercise Affects Body Temperature

II. Introductory Statement
The learner will analyze the information gathered from a sample population to determine whether or not activity changes the body temperature.

III.

Math Skills	Science Processes
a. Practicing	a. Observing
b. Computing percent	b. Classifying
c. Charting	c. Measuring
d. Graphing	d. Predicting and estimating
e. Measuring	e. Controlling variables and data
	f. Recording data
	g. Analyzing and generalizing

IV. Materials
One large class chart
400 m measured course
Three colored markers and pencils
Five thermometers—Celsius
Isoprophyl (rubbing) alcohol
Cup
Student worksheets, pages 39-40

V. Key Question
"Does the heat you feel after exercise indicate a rise in true body temerature?"

VII. Management Suggestions
1. Sterilize thermometers in isoprophyl alcohol.
2. Students should be divided into three groups of five students:
   Experimental group 1
   Experimental group 2
   Control group

VIII. Procedure
1. Group students (five per group).
2. Take temperature of each student in each group, record on student data sheet.
3. Have the control group sit.
4. Have experimental group 1 walk a 400 m lap.
5. Have experimental group 2 run a 400 m lap.
6. Record temperatures at the end of activity.
   a. First, runners
   b. Second, walkers
   c. Third, sitters
7. Record and graph on student chart.
8. Construct class data sheet, average, etc.

X. Discussion
1. What effect did exercise have on the body temperature overall?
2. Can you identify variations in body temperature?
3. Analyze and discuss class average vs. individual temperatures.

XI. Extension
1. Students can take their temperatures at given times during the day and night.
2. Prepare a temperature cycle per student.
3. Graph individual averages and compare to average 98.6°. Chart variations.

From Head to Toe

AM I YOUR TYPE?

I. Topic Area

Blood Typing

II. Introductory Statement

In studying the human body processes, one of the basic and most essential is the circulatory system. One of the most important aspects of this system is finding out what your blood type is.

III. Math Skills

a. Charting
b. Using ratio/proportion
c. Figuring differences

Science Processes

a. Observing
b. Classifying
c. Predicting
d. Estimating

IV. Materials

Alcohol pad or cotton ball
Lancet
Toothpicks (two)
Anti-A and Anti-B Glutens
Hemo-Pad
Paper towel—about 12" x 18"
Student worksheets, pages 41-43

V. Key Question

"What is my blood type? Why do we have to know what our blood type is?"

VI. Background Information

1. Blood typing kits are available but must be ordered at least six weeks prior to testing.
2. Kits and materials that aren't used can be kept and used the following year without any apparent loss in accuracy of results.
3. Keep ammonia inhalents handy.
4. Allow plenty of ventilation flow and low heat. (Alcohol reminds students of doctor's offices.)
5. Have students pick up all materials prior to testing. DO NOT ALLOW STUDENTS TO MOVE AROUND IMMEDIATELY AFTER TESTS: FIVE TO TEN MINUTES IN-SEAT TIME RECOMMENDED.
6. Explain and demonstrate procedures thoroughly prior to testing. (One day seems to work.)
7. DO NOT minimize amount of pain. Let students know there will be some; however, it is nothing they haven't experienced before. This cuts down on students overreacting on testing day.
8. Permission sheets sent home and returned by testing day.

VII. Management Suggestions

1. Lay out materials before activity. Have students make a materials list before testing.
2. Have a sequential arrangement of materials as they will be needed.
3. To save you time, have two non-participants administer anti-glutens as students need them. This frees the teacher for observation.
4. Prior to test, go over all possible results pictorially that students could have occur. (You will still have to confirm results.)
5. All procedures should be gone over prior to testing, including the materials needed: hygiene, actual testing, reading of results, clean up, follow up, etc.

VIII. Procedure

1. Lay out materials on paper toweling.
2. Tear wrapper from handle end of lancet—do not expose tip to air.
3. Remove wrapper from alcohol pad.
4. Sterilize tip of index finger with alcohol pad, allow to air dry.
5. Apply force with your thumb to base of first joint of index finger. Place pad of middle finger on cuticle of index finger. Press.
6. Taking lancet between index finger and thumb of your working hand, line up tip with pad of index finger. With a short, forceful jab poke one hole in index finger tip.
7. Blot first drop of blood on alcohol pad. Place lancet on paper towel for later disposal. Using thumb, squeeze one drop of blood from fingertip—place drop in Circle A. Place a second drop in Circle B. Raise hand to receive anti-glutens. Place alcohol pad on puncture and hold in place with your thumb.
8. After receiving Anti A-Anti B solutions, stir Anti A circle thoroughly with side of toothpick. Be sure to spread mixture out to fill entire circle. Discard toothpick onto paper towel. Get second toothpick and repeat operation for Anti B circle. Discard toothpick onto paper towel.
9. Pick up hemo-card and gently rock for about one to two minutes. Set card down, watch results.
10. Record blood type.
    (1) If after stirring, rocking, etc., A and B remain the same—you have blood Type O.
    (2) If A circle shows clotting and circle B does not—you are Type A.
    (3) If circle B clots and A remains unchanged—you have Type B blood.
    (4) If both circle A and B clot—you have type AB blood.

Take A Breather!
PERSONAL LUNG CAPACITY

I. Topic Area
Lung Capacity

II. Introductory Statement
This activity allows children to become aware of factors that affect lung capacity.

III. Math Skills
a. Averaging
b. Charting
c. Solving for an unknown

Science Processes
a. Controlling data and variables
b. Applying
c. Generalizing

IV. Materials
Centimeter tapes (one per two students)
Common nine-inch balloons (one package of twelve per two students)
Student worksheets, pages 44-48

V. Key Question
"What are some factors that affect lung capacity?"

VI. Technical Information
1. Lung capacity is measured by determining the volume of air the lungs can hold. Therefore, instead of referring to these as "capacity" measurements, we call them "volume" measurements.
2. The circumference measurement is not a measurements of volume; however, it does give an indication of volume.
3. Definitions:
   Tidal air volume—amount of breath lungs contain during normal breathing (not measurable by balloon test, so not included during testing)
   Reserve air volume—amount of breath that can be forced out of lungs after normal exhalation
   Vital air volume—maximum amount of air that lungs can hold

VII. Management Suggestions
1. Allow one week for total activity by following the suggested schedule in Procedure, part VIII.
2. Students should work in pairs with one as interviewer and one as recorder.

VIII. Procedure
Day One (approximately one hour)
1. Suggestions for pre-activity discussion:
   a. Does everyone breathe exactly alike? (Define inhale and exhale.)
   b. Count how many times you inhale normally in one minute. Compare with others.
   c. Describe what happens when you inhale. Describe what happens when you exhale.
   d. What happens when you try to take in more air after inhaling normally? (Your lungs fill to full capacity and your chest expands.)
   e. Is it possible to exhale more air than you inhale? Why? (Yes, because there's air left in your lungs after normally exhaling.)
   f. Discuss and define tidal, reserve, and vital air volume. (See Technical information. *Warning:* A lot of explanation and demonstration is involved in defining reserve air volume. Explain that reserve air is that which is left in the lungs after *normal* exhalation. Many students will unwittingly take a short breath before forcing out all their air.)
   g. Do you know anyone who might have trouble doing some of these breathing exercises? Why? (Write students' answers on board. Factors that students might suggest are age, sex, exercise habits, weight and smoking habits. If students don't suggest these, direct discussion toward recognizing them as factors.)
   h. Restate Key Question: "What are some factors that affect lung capacity?"
2. Hand out a student interview sheet (student worksheet page 45) on which each student will do a practice interview.
3. Perform the following procedure on a selected student. All other students observe and record the results. (Note: Do each step in the procedure as precisely as possible, since this is what the students will have to do on their own.)
   a. Record the selected student's response to the interview questions at top of interview sheet.
   b. Perform lung capacity test. (Note: Make sure you inflate balloon twice before taking measurement so balloon's resistance is lessened.)
   c. Lung Capacity Tests:
      Reserve air test—Student exhales reserve air into balloon. Pinch balloon's nozzle. With cm tape, measure circumference of inflated balloon at widest point. Record on sheet for Trial #1. Repeat twice more for reserve air volume.
      Vital air test—Do same procedure three times, determining vital air volume. Record these results.
   d. Compute averages on each sheet.
4. Choose student pairs.
5. Give each pair two balloons, one cm tape and two interview sheets so they may practice on each other. Give assistance where needed.
6. Discuss any problems.

From Head to Toe

Days Two and Three

Assign the above tasks to be performed on a varied group of at least four people outside of class. (Stress the importance of selecting four very different people to interview. Example—a large person, a smoker, an old person and a young person.)

Days Four and Five (approximately one hour each day)

1. Have students average the results on each sheet.
2. Hand out Master Data Sheet (student worksheet page 46) to each student pair. Have them tally in the appropriate color code the averages for each interview sheet.
3. Compile results from all Master Data Sheets on a similar Class Data Sheet (tagboard, overhead or chalkboard).
4. (For seventh or eighth grade or advanced elementary.) Using student worksheet, compute the actual volume from the circumference figure.

IX. **Discussion**

1. Interpret the charts to arrive at as many conclusions as possible.
2. Which factors affect a person's lung capacity? (non-smoking, exercising, etc.)
3. What factors benefit lung capacity? Compare them. (Exercise may be more important than non-smoking.)
4. What factors are detrimental to lung capacity? Compare. (Smoking, old age; smoking may be more detrimental, in most cases.)
5. Which type of lung capacity is most affected by each factor? (See results of Master Data Sheet.)

XI. **Extension**

1. Explain how lung capacity is related to our daily living habits. (exercise, smoking, etc.)
2. As we grow older, how can we keep our lung capacity at its maximum? (By developing good living habits that are beneficial to lung capacity.)

14

From Head to Toe

You Take My Breath Away

I. Topic Area
Respiration

II. Introductory Statement
All the activities of a living organism require energy. Human activities such as walking, running, breathing and even sleeping require different amounts of energy. Some, such as sleeping, require very little energy, while others, such as running, require much energy. Those activities requiring a great deal of energy are called *Strenuous Activities*. In this investigation you are going to use normal respiratory rates as a method to determine which of two activities is more strenuous.

III. Math Skills / Science Processes

Math Skills	Science Processes
a. Counting	a. Observing
b. Averaging	b. Hypothesizing
c. Measuring time	c. Recording data
d. Graphing	d. Interpreting data
e. Estimating	e. Generalizing

IV. Materials
A bicycle and a chair
A clock or stopwatch
Student worksheets, pages 49-50

V. Key Question
"Which form of exercise is more strenuous, riding a bicycle or jogging?"

Grabber—Use Lycopodium and an alcohol burner to create a flash, and relate to oxygen utilization in the breathing process and respiration in the cell.
1. Place match to Lycopodium flour (it won't burn) and say: "Please note the lack of reaction by the Lycopodium to the heat source."
2. Toss Lycopodium onto an alcohol burner (this will result in a flash explosion). Use a small amount—1 teaspoon maximum. Say: "Please note
   a. "The Lycopodium is the same
   b. "The flame source is the same
   c. "What factor is different?"

3. Answer:
   a. The oxygen supply—it combines more effectively with the Lycopodium.

VIII. Procedure
1. Determine your normal respiratory rate:
   a. Count how many times you breathe in one minute
   b. Repeat two more times (total of 3).
   c. Find your average normal respiratory rate.
2. Ride a bicycle for 5 minutes without stopping
3. Stop riding and immediately determine your respiratory rate. (You will need to have a partner to help you count)
4. Record this data on a data table.
5. Sit down and rest until your respiratory rate returns to normal and stays normal for at least 3 minutes.
6. Now go jogging for 5 minutes without stopping.
7. Stop jogging and immediately determine your respiratory rate.
8. Record this data on your data table.
9. Using your data table and your average normal respiratory rate, make a bar graph that shows which activity is more strenuous.

IX. Discussion
1. What are some of the variables that could affect respiration rates? (physical condition, age, sex, smoking, etc.)
2. What would be another way to measure and compare the strenuous nature of an activity? (heart rate)
3. Predict which would be more strenuous, swimming for 5 minutes or roller skating for 5 minutes? *Why?*
4. How could we measure and compare the efficiency of bicycle riding and jogging? (distance divided by respiratory rate)

XI. Extension
1. Use a chair stepping exercise indoors as a substitute for the bicycle.
2. Compare the respiratory rate activities done before lunch; and the same activities done after lunch.

From Head to Toe

How Do You Measure Up?

"Estimate your measurements in metrics, then use a tape measure to find your actual measurements."

Put in your own face!

Around head ____ est. ____ actual

Ear length ____ est. ____ actual

smile ____ est. ____ actual

Nose length ____ est. ____ actual

Height ____ est. ____ actual

Around neck ____ est. ____ actual

Chest ____ est. ____ actual

Arm length ____ est. ____ actual

chest

waist ____ est. ____ actual

Thumb length ____ est. ____ actual

Around ring finger ____ est. ____ actual

Around little finger ____ est. ____ actual

Leg length ____ est. ____ actual

Width of calf ____ est. ____ actual

Around Big Toe ____ est. ____ actual

Big Toe length ____ est. ____ actual

Foot length ____ est. ____ actual

From Head to Toe

METRIC MASTER

height _____

elbow to middle finger _____

knee to floor _____

leg length _____

circumference of neck _____

circumference of chest _____

palm _____

foot width _____

circumference of big toe _____

circumference of head _____

circumference of wrist _____

circumference of arm _____

nose to fingertip _____

foot length _____

circumference of ankle _____

regular step _____

large step _____

gigantic step _____

handspan _____

thumb _____

pinkie _____

middle finger _____

index finger _____

weight _____

shoe width _____

shoe length _____

shoe weight _____

circumference of calf _____

circumference of ankle _____

waist _____

_____ _____
Signed

_____ _____
Date   Age

I promise that all the above measurements are accurate to the best of my ability.

SEAL OF APPROVAL

2.

1		26	10	51	20	76	30
2	1	27		52		77	
3		28	11	53	21	78	31
4		29		54		79	
5	2	30	12	55	22	80	32
6		31		56		81	
7		32		57		82	
8	3	33	13	58	23	83	33
9		34		59		84	
10	4	35		60		85	
11		36	14	61	24	86	34
12		37		62		87	
13	5	38	15	63	25	88	35
14		39		64		89	
15	6	40	16	65		90	
16		41		66	26	91	YARD 36
17		42		67		92	
18	7	43	17	68	27	93	37
19		44		69		94	
20	8	45		70		95	
21		46	18	71	28	96	38
22		47		72		97	
23	9	48	19	73	29	98	
24		49		74		99	39
25		50		75		100 METER	

TAPE MEASURE

3.

From Head to Toe

What is the Average Student Like?

Mark Boy or Girl.   Give your Best answers!

1. B G	Age		18. B G	Favorite TV Show	
2. B G	Height		19. B G	Hours per day spent watching T.V.	
3. B G	Weight		20. B G	All-time Favorite Movie	
4. B G	Eye Color		21. B G	Jean Brand	
5. B G	Hair Color		22. B G	Shoe Size	
6. B G	Hair type	curly straight wavy	23. B G	Best Video Game	
7. B G	Hair length	long medium short	24. B G	How do you get to school?	
8. B G	Freckles	yes no	25. B G	Shoe Brand	
9. B G	Glasses	yes no	26. B G	Hobby	
10. B G	Favorite Subject		27. B G	Holiday	
11. B G	Most Disliked Subject		28. B G	Favorite Actor	
12. B G	Favorite Color		29. B G	Favorite Actress	
13. B G	Food		30. B G	Future Occupation	
14. B G	Lucky Number		31. B G	Pet	
15. B G	Gum Flavor		32. B G	Brand of Shampoo	
16. B G	Candy Bar		33. B G	Horoscope	
17. B G	Sport		34. B G	Favorite Song	

4.

From Head to Toe

SAMPLE GRAPHS

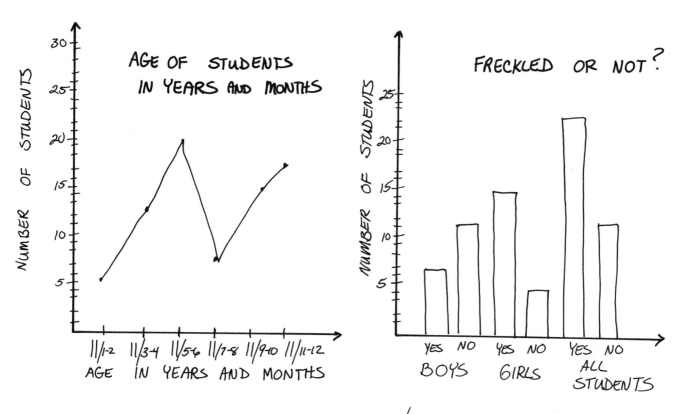

AGE OF STUDENTS IN YEARS AND MONTHS

Number of Students (y-axis): 5, 10, 15, 20, 25, 30

AGE IN YEARS AND MONTHS (x-axis): 11/1-2 11/3-4 11/5-6 11/7-8 11/9-10 11/11-12

FRECKLED OR NOT?

Number of Students (y-axis): 5, 10, 15, 20, 25

YES NO — BOYS
YES NO — GIRLS
YES NO — ALL STUDENTS

Be Creative!

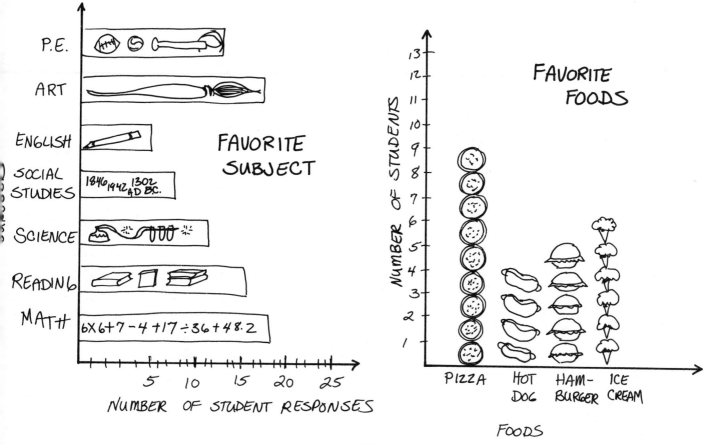

FAVORITE SUBJECT

P.E.
ART
ENGLISH
SOCIAL STUDIES   1846 1942 1302 AD B.C.
SCIENCE
READING
MATH   6 X 6 + 7 - 4 + 17 ÷ 36 + 48.2

NUMBER OF STUDENT RESPONSES: 5 10 15 20 25

FAVORITE FOODS

Number of Students (y-axis): 1, 2, 3, 4, 5, 6, 7, 8, 9, 10, 11, 12, 13

FOODS (x-axis): PIZZA HOT DOG HAMBURGER ICE CREAM

5.

From Head to Toe

_____ NAME

COLOR of HAIR

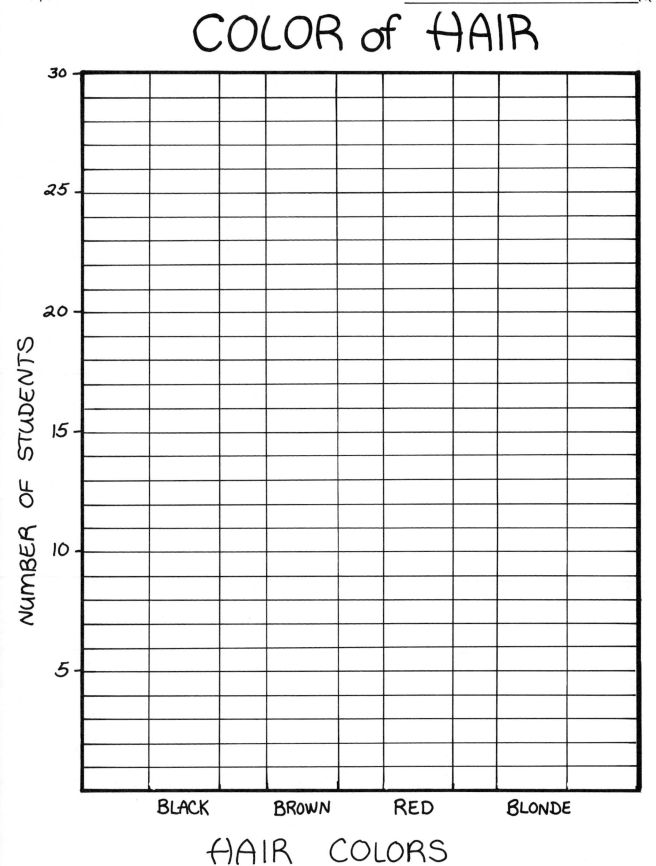

NUMBER OF STUDENTS

30 —
25 —
20 —
15 —
10 —
5 —

BLACK   BROWN   RED   BLONDE

HAIR COLORS

From Head to Toe

How Average Are You?

Name _____

 Last   First   Middle Initial

          Pre   Post

Weight _____   _____   _____   _____

         Kilograms   pounds   Kilograms   pounds

Height _____   _____   _____   _____

            cm   inches   cm   inches

EYE COLOR _____.

HAIR COLOR _____

7.

From Head to Toe

ARE YOU MEAN?

_____NAME

ESTIMATE YOUR MEASUREMENT IN CM, THEN MEASURE TO FIND YOUR ACTUAL MEASUREMENTS. RECORD AND FIND THE DIFFERENCE.

MEASURE:	ESTIMATE	ACTUAL MEASUREMENT	DIFFERENCE + or −
1. EAR LENGTH			
2. NOSE LENGTH			
3. AROUND NECK			
4. SMILE			
5. AROUND HEAD			
6. HEIGHT			
7. CHEST			
8. LEG LENGTH			
9. FOOT LENGTH			
10. BIG TOE LENGTH			
11. CALF WIDTH			
12. WAIST			
13. ARM LENGTH			
14. THUMB LENGTH			
15. AROUND LITTLE FINGER			
16. AROUND RING FINGER			
17. AROUND BIG TOE			

I'M MEAN!

TOTAL DIFFERENCE

÷ 17

AVERAGE DIFFERENCE

8.

From Head to Toe

_____ NAME

CORPUS All AROUND US

USE YOUR DRAWN BODY OUTLINE. MEASURE ALL LENGTHS IN CM AND RECORD YOUR MEASUREMENTS.

	CM MEASUREMENT		CM MEASUREMENT
HAND SPAN (FINGER TO THUMB)		DISTANCE FROM RIGHT EAR TO LEFT EAR	
HEEL TO TOE OF RIGHT-FOOT		SHOULDER JOINT TO HIP JOINT	
WRIST TO ELBOW		WRIST TO SHOULDER	
ELBOW TO SHOULDER		SHOULDER JOINT TO TOP OF HEAD	
BASE OF HEAD TO BASE OF SPINE		TOP OF HEAD TO CENTER OF EAR	
KNEE TO ANKLE		CENTER OF EAR TO JAW	
HIP JOINT TO ANKLE		CENTER OF EAR TO BRIDGE OF NOSE	
SHOULDER JOINT TO CLAVICLE		CENTER OF EAR TO BACK OF HEAD	
TOP OF HEAD TO POINT OF JAW		CENTER OF EAR TO SHOULDER	
HIP JOINT TO KNEE		WIDTH OF BALL OF FOOT	
FINGER LENGTHS 1 2 3 4 5		TOE LENGTHS 1 2 3 4 5	

USE A TAPE MEASURE OR A RULER

TRACE YOUR BODY OUTLINE ACCURATELY ON A LARGE PIECE OF PAPER. PUT MASKING TAPE AROUND THE EDGES. MEASURE AND RECORD TO THE NEAREST CM.

9.

©1986 AIMS Education Foundation

From Head to Toe

Golden Proportion

_____ NAME

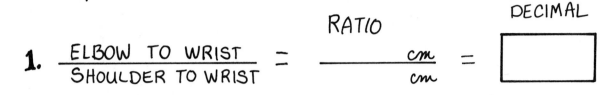

Use Your Data From "Corpus All Around Us."
Compare Lengths And Make Ratios.

RATIO DECIMAL

1. $\dfrac{\text{ELBOW TO WRIST}}{\text{SHOULDER TO WRIST}}$ = $\dfrac{\underline{\hspace{2cm}} cm}{\underline{\hspace{2cm}} cm}$ = ☐

2. $\dfrac{\text{KNEE TO ANKLE}}{\text{HIP TO ANKLE}}$ = $\dfrac{\underline{\hspace{2cm}} cm}{\underline{\hspace{2cm}} cm}$ = ☐

3. $\dfrac{\text{HIP TO BOTTOM OF FOOT}}{\substack{\text{TOP OF HEAD TO BOTTOM} \\ \text{OF FOOT}}}$ = $\dfrac{\underline{\hspace{2cm}} cm}{\underline{\hspace{2cm}} cm}$ = ☐

DECIMAL TOTAL = ☐

DECIMAL AVERAGE = ☐

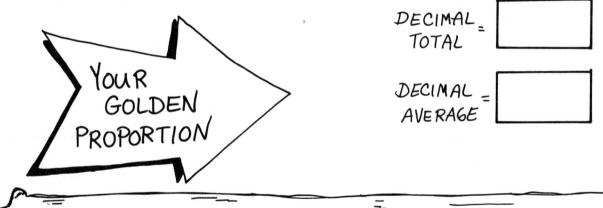

YOUR GOLDEN PROPORTION

MEASURE YOUR THIGH BONE (FEMUR) _____ cm
THEN :

BOYS (FEMUR) _____ cm X 1.88 + 81.31 cm = _____ cm

GIRLS (FEMUR) _____ cm X 1.945 + 72.84 cm = _____ cm

HOW DOES YOUR ANSWER COMPARE WITH YOUR HEIGHT?

10.

From Head to Toe

Ye Olde Records for Dem Bones of

NAME

Skull

	cm
1. NASAL TO OCCIPITAL (BACK OF HEAD)	1. _____
2. TOP OF FOREHEAD TO BASE OF LOWER JAW	2. _____
3. POINT OF CHIN TO BACK OF JAW	3. _____
4. BACK OF JAW TO BACK OF HEAD	4. _____

Shoulder Bone

5. COLLAR BONE FROM STERNUM TO SHOULDER	5. _____

Shoulder Blade

6. FROM SHOULDER TO INNER EDGE	6. _____
7. FROM TOP TO BOTTOM	7. _____
8. FROM INNER TO OUTER EDGE AT BASE	8. _____
9. WIDTH OF NARROW PORTION OF SHOULDER	9. _____

Arm

10. UPPER ARM FROM BEND AT SHOULDER TO ELBOW	10. _____
11. LOWER ARM FROM BEND OF ELBOW TO BEND OF WRIST	11. _____

Fingers
(measure with fingers bent)

	FINGER JOINTS	cm
12. INDEX	12. 1st	_____
	2nd	_____
	3rd	_____
13. MIDDLE	13. 1st	_____
	2nd	_____
	3rd	_____
14. RING	14. 1st	_____
	2nd	_____
	3rd	_____
15. LITTLE	15. 1st	_____
	2nd	_____
	3rd	_____
16. THUMB	16. 1st	_____
	2nd	_____

Palm
(measure from knuckle to wrist bend)

17. INDEX	17. _____
18. MIDDLE	18. _____
19. RING	19. _____
20. LITTLE	20. _____
21. THUMB	21. _____

Wrist

22. FROM BEND OF WRIST TO BEND OF PALM	22. _____

Spine

23. NECK - FROM BASE OF SKULL TO SHOULDER	23. _____
24. SPINE FROM SHOULDER TO BEND IN WAIST	24. _____

page 1.

From Head to Toe

Ye Olde Records for Dem Bones

of

NAME

Pelvis   cm

25. WIDTH   25. _____
26. LENGTH FROM TOP OF
    HIP BONE TO BALL/SOCKET   26. _____
    PLUS ONE HAND WIDTH
27. SPACE FOR ILIUM/SPINE   27. _____
    CONNECTION EQUALS ¼
    TOTAL WIDTH
28. WIDTH OF LOWER PELVIS   28. _____
    EQUALS ½ UPPER WIDTH
29. SPACE BETWEEN LOWER   29. _____
    FLANGE = ¼ LOWER WIDTH

Upper Leg

30. FROM BALL/SOCKET TO   30. _____
    KNEE BEND
31. BALL/SOCKET EQUALS   31. _____
    ¾ HAND WIDTH

Knee Cap

32. MEASURE ACROSS IN   32. _____
    3 DIFFERENT AREAS

Lower Leg

33. FROM KNEE BEND TO   33. _____
    ANKLE BEND PLUS
    2 FINGER WIDTHS

Toes   cm
measure with toes bent

33. BIG   33. 1st _____
                     2nd _____
34. SECOND   34. 1st _____
                     2nd _____
35. THIRD   35. 1st _____
                     2nd _____
36. FOURTH   36. 1st _____
                     2nd _____
37. LITTLE   37. 1st _____
                     2nd _____

Foot
(measure from bend of
toes to bend of foot)

38. BIG   38. _____
39. SECOND   39. _____
40. THIRD   40. _____
41. FOURTH   41. _____
42. LITTLE   42. _____

Ankle

43. FROM BEND OF   43. _____
    FOOT TO APEX OF
    HEEL

Dr. Bones

M.D. OF
BONEOLOGY

page 2.

12.

From Head to Toe

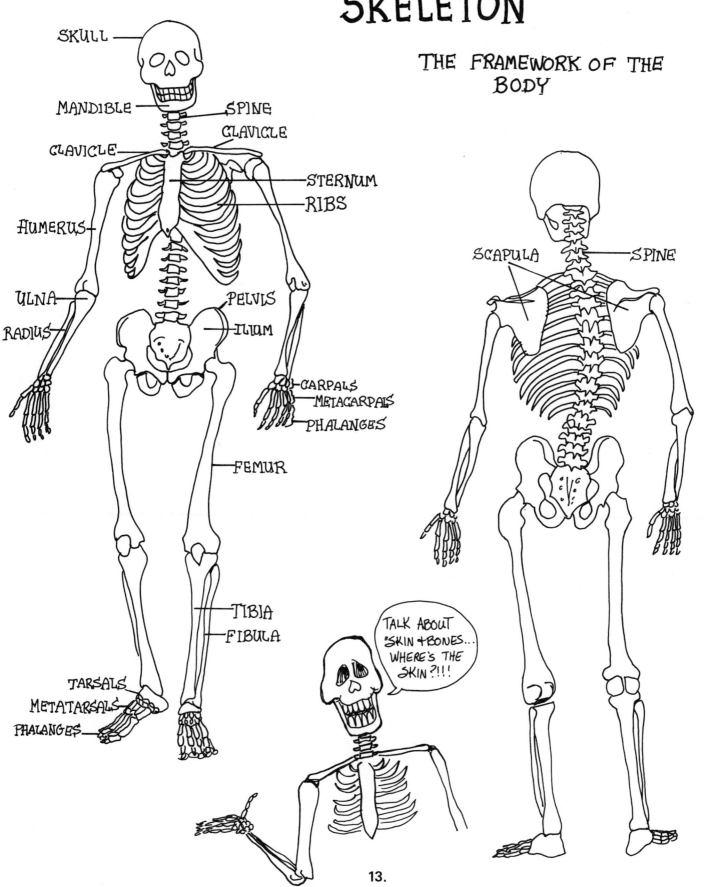

"DEM BONES"
SKELETON

THE FRAMEWORK OF THE BODY

SKULL

MANDIBLE

SPINE

CLAVICLE

CLAVICLE

STERNUM

RIBS

HUMERUS

SCAPULA

SPINE

ULNA

PELVIS

RADIUS

ILIUM

CARPALS

METACARPALS

PHALANGES

FEMUR

TIBIA

FIBULA

TALK ABOUT "SKIN + BONES... WHERE'S THE SKIN?!!!

TARSALS

METATARSALS

PHALANGES

13.

From Head to Toe

'DEM BONES'

SIDE VIEW OF SKULL

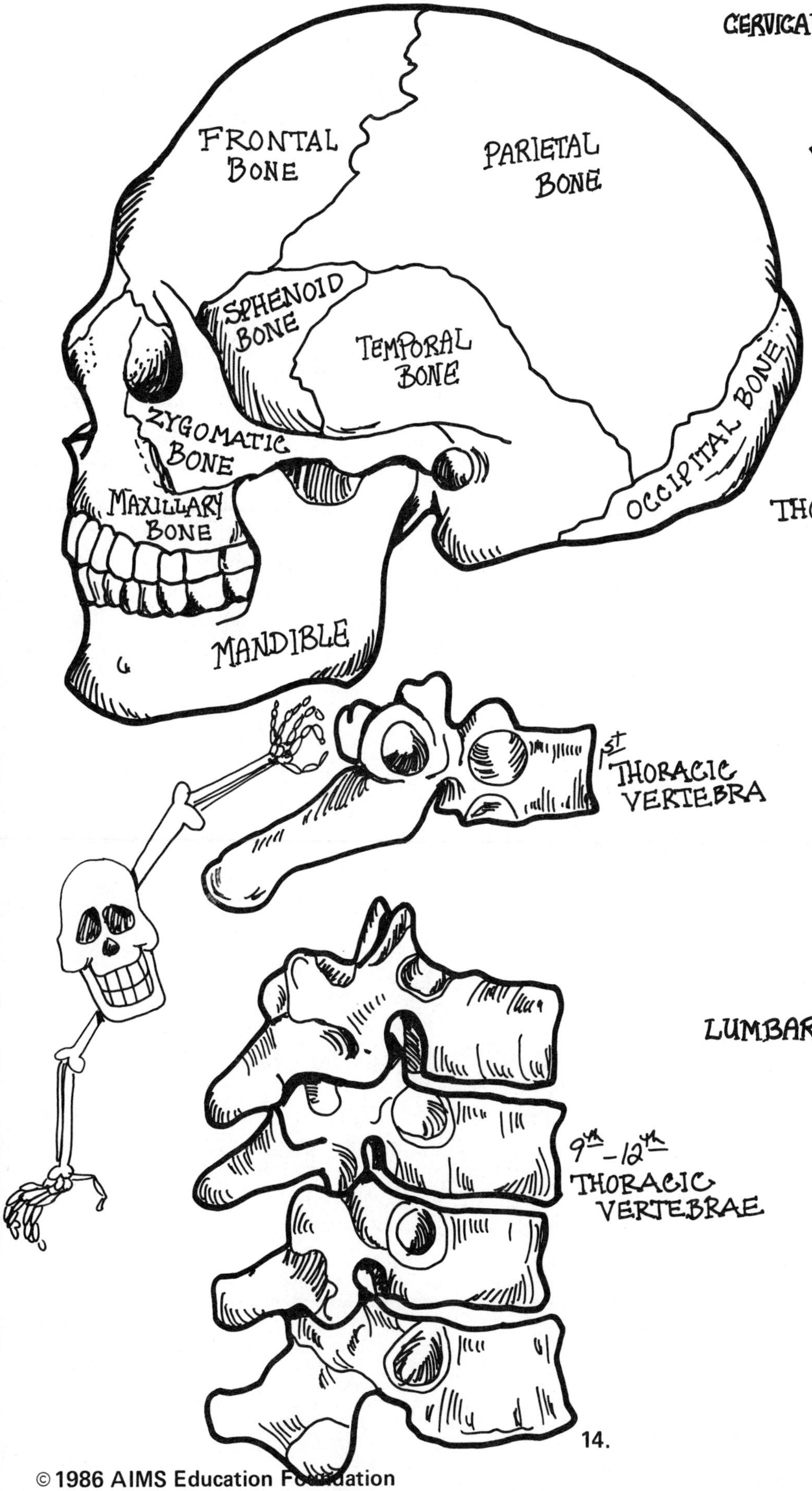

SPINE

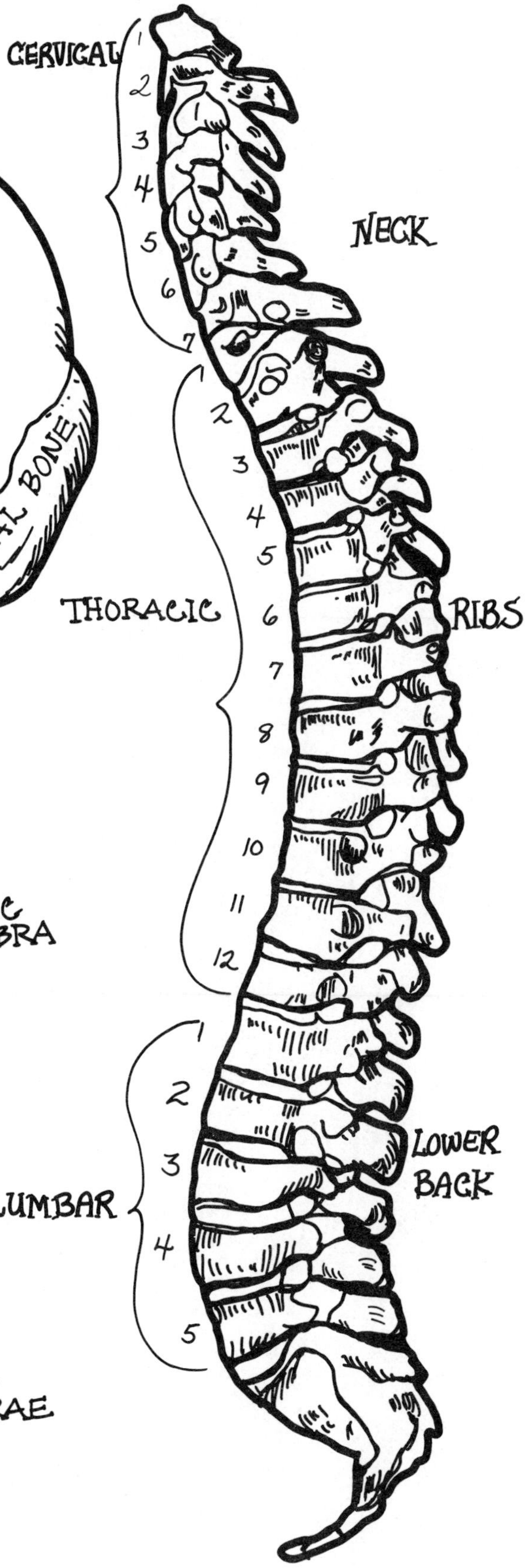

FRONTAL BONE

PARIETAL BONE

SPHENOID BONE

TEMPORAL BONE

OCCIPITAL BONE

ZYGOMATIC BONE

MAXILLARY BONE

MANDIBLE

CERVICAL

1
2
3
4
5
6
7

NECK

THORACIC

1
2
3
4
5
6
7
8
9
10
11
12

RIBS

1st THORACIC VERTEBRA

9th - 12th THORACIC VERTEBRAE

LUMBAR

1
2
3
4
5

LOWER BACK

14.

From Head to Toe

SHOULDER UNIT   'DEM BONES'

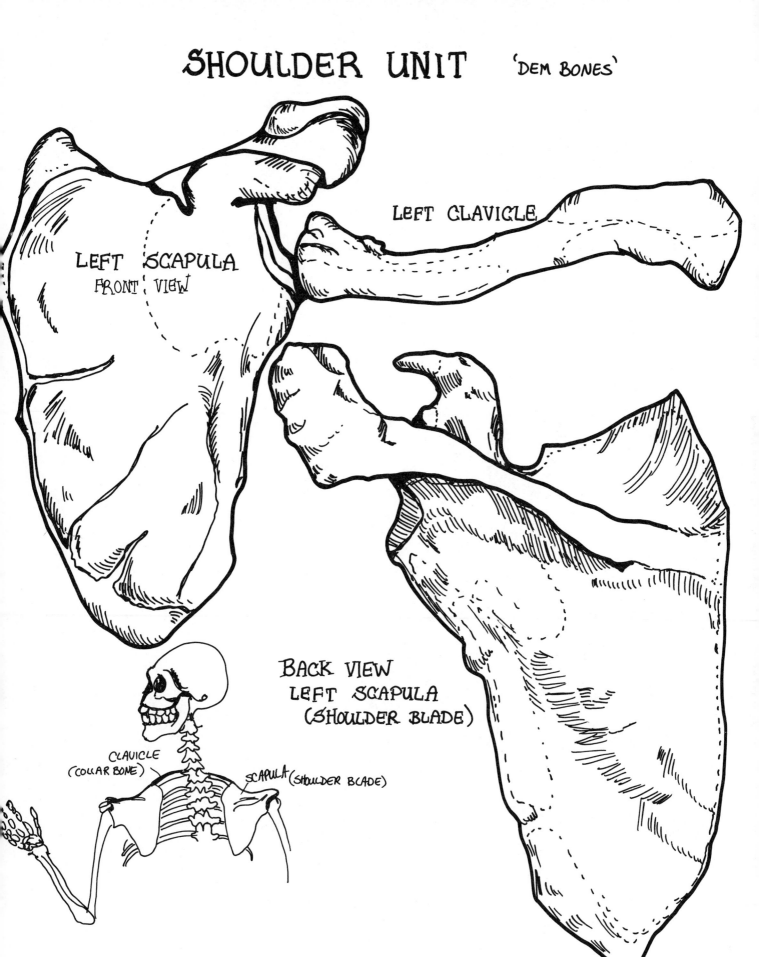

LEFT CLAVICLE

LEFT SCAPULA
FRONT VIEW

BACK VIEW
LEFT SCAPULA
(SHOULDER BLADE)

CLAVICLE
(COLLAR BONE)

SCAPULA (SHOULDER BLADE)

15.

From Head to Toe

RIBS

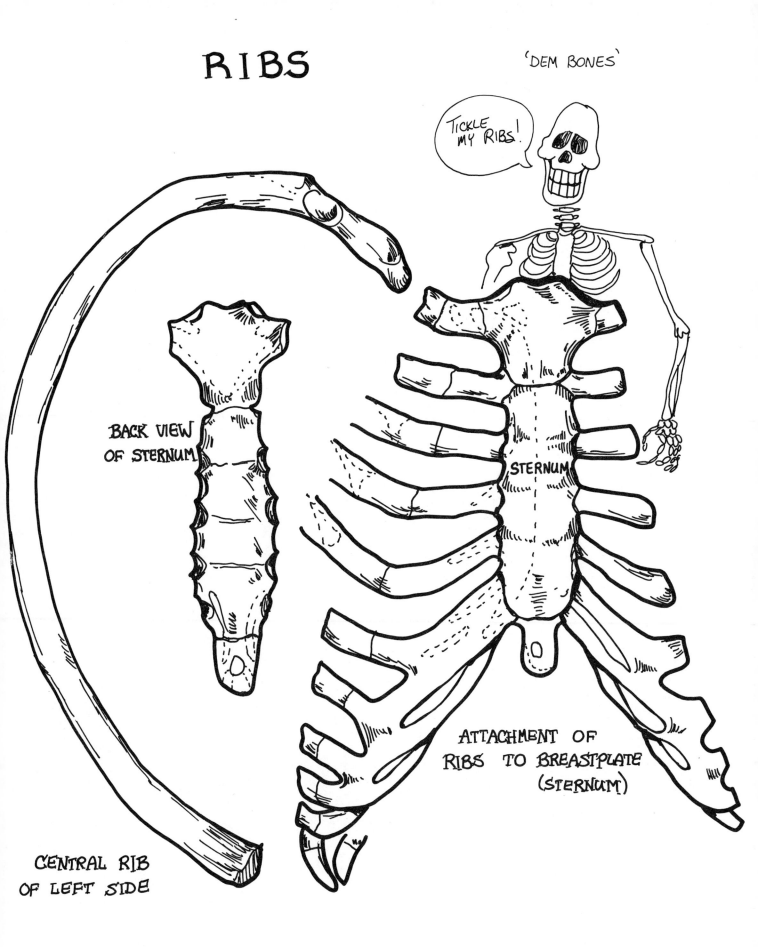

16.

From Head to Toe

Bones Of The Left Hand
Palm Down

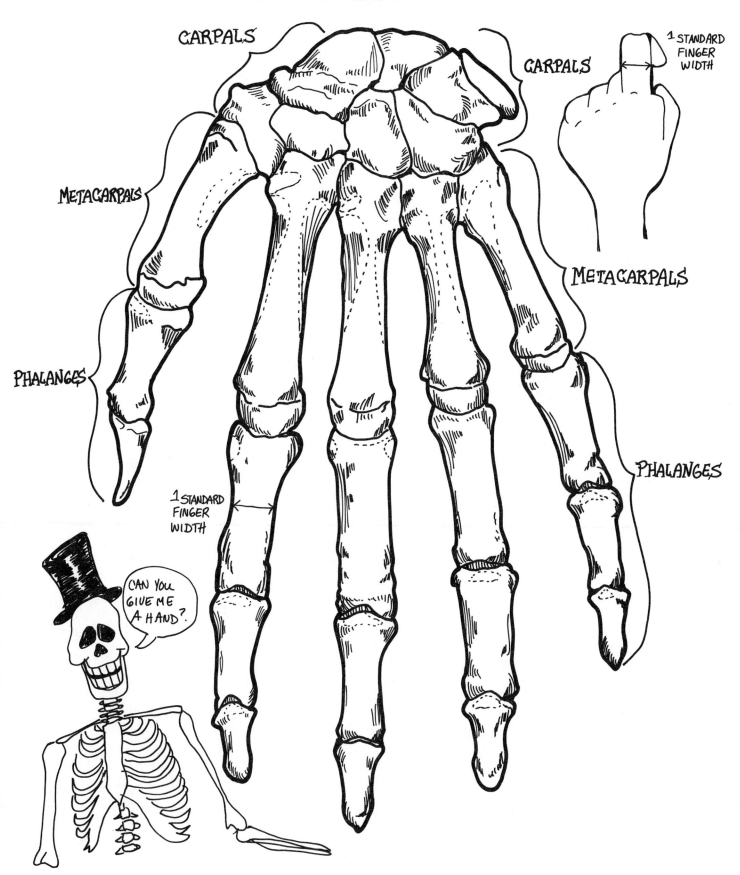

CARPALS

CARPALS

METACARPALS

METACARPALS

PHALANGES

PHALANGES

1 STANDARD FINGER WIDTH

1 STANDARD FINGER WIDTH

CAN YOU GIVE ME A HAND?

17.

From Head to Toe

BONES of the LEFT ARM

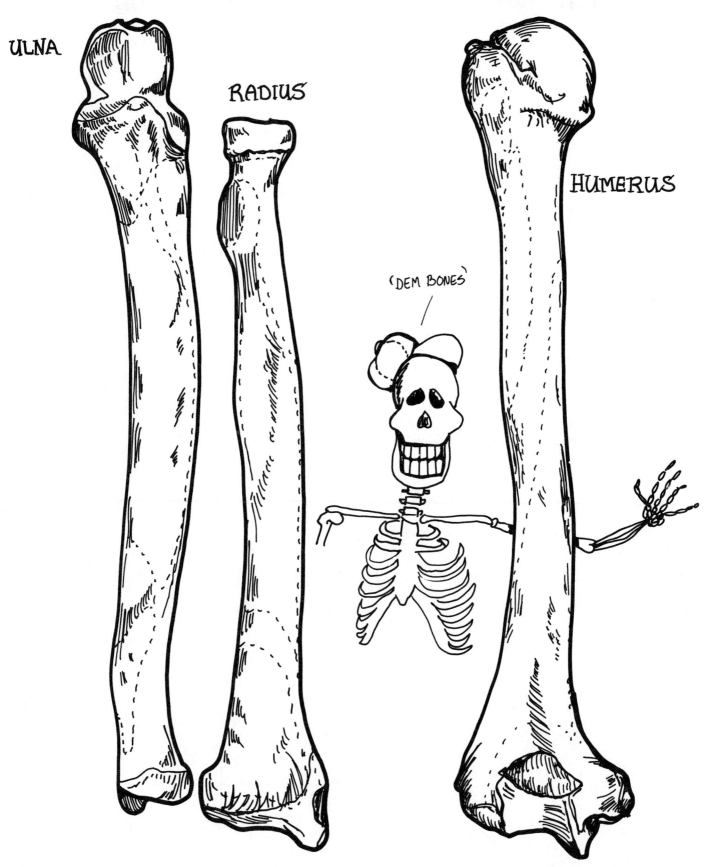

ULNA

RADIUS

HUMERUS

'DEM BONES'

From Head to Toe

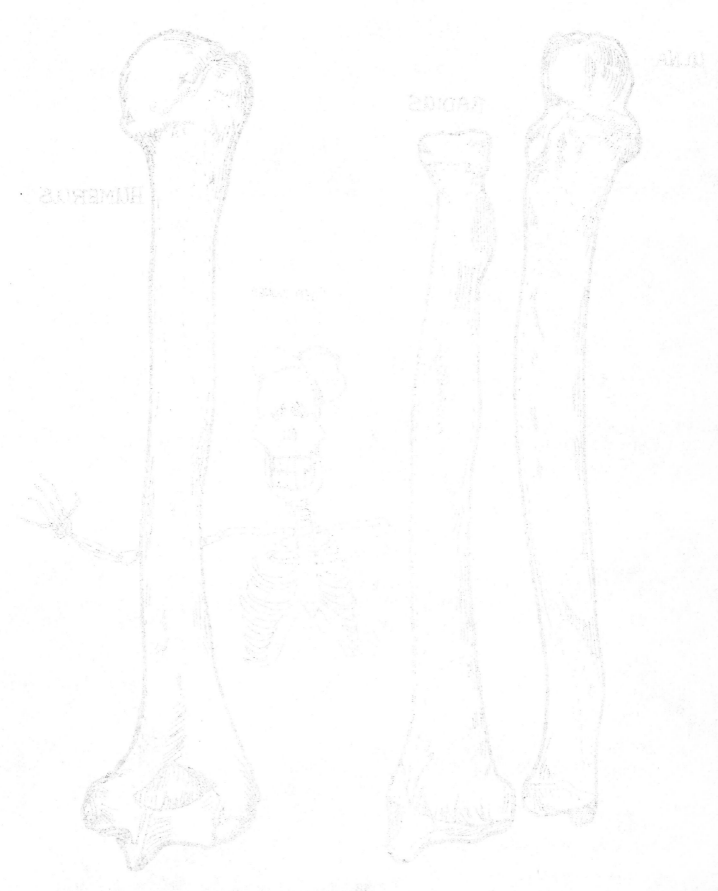

BONES OF RIGHT FOOT

BONES OF RIGHT LEG

'DEM BONES

LOWER LEG

UPPER LEG

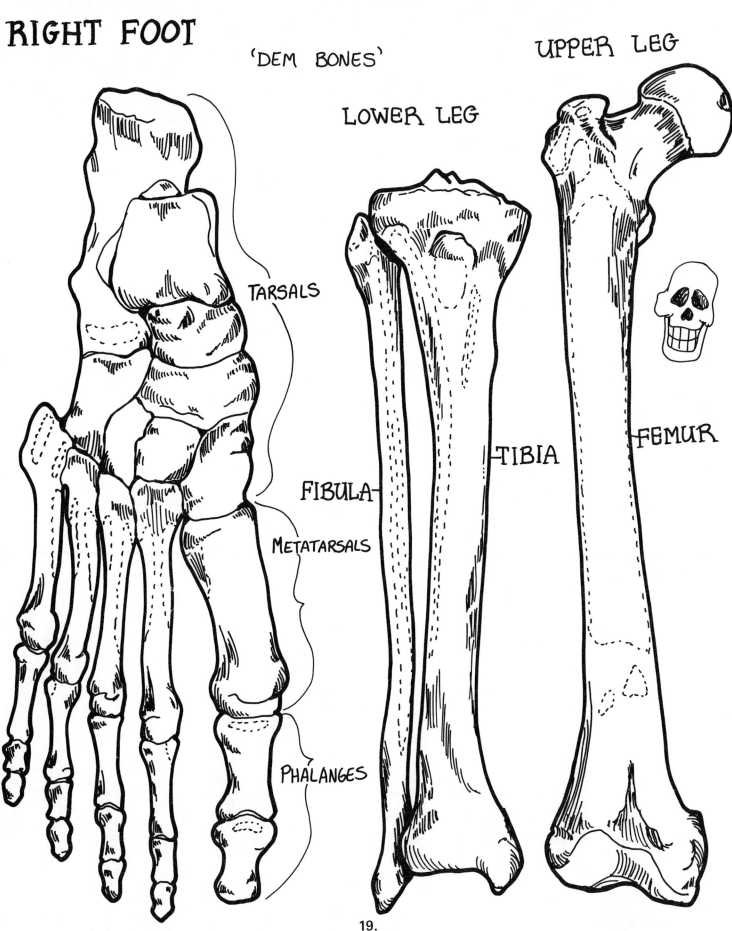

TARSALS

METATARSALS

PHALANGES

FIBULA

TIBIA

FEMUR

From Head to Toe

PELVIS

'DEM BONES'

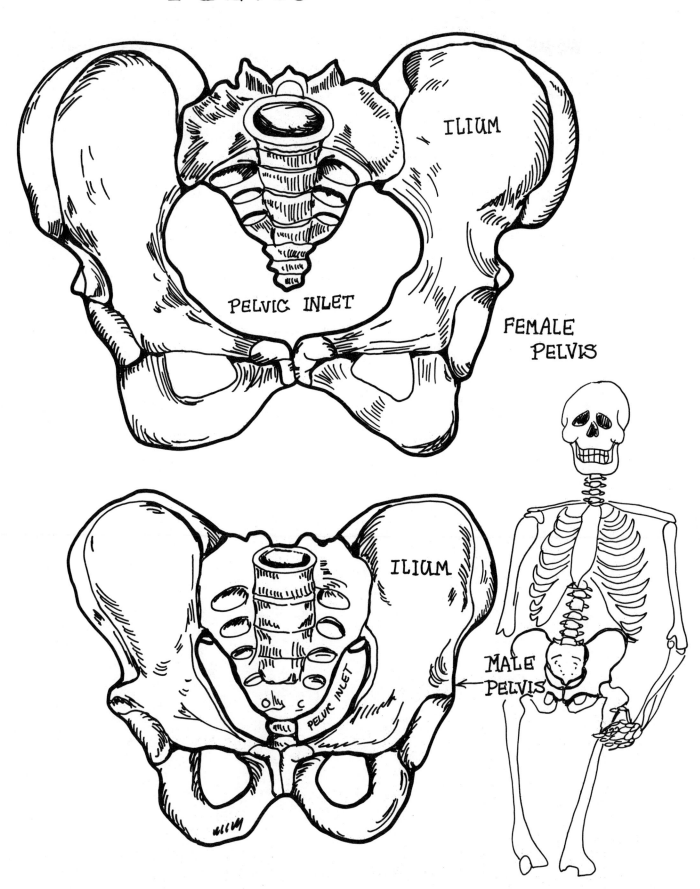

ILIUM

PELVIC INLET

FEMALE PELVIS

ILIUM

PELVIC INLET

MALE PELVIS

20.

From Head to Toe

ARM YOURSELF

AGE _____
GRADE _____
SEX _____

NAME

PRACTICE &
TRY AGAIN!
↓

	TRIAL 1	TRIAL 2
1. NUMBER OF PUSHUPS COMPLETED		
2. PERCENTILE RANKING %		
3. NUMBER OF PUSHUPS CLASS AVERAGE		
4. PERCENTILE RANKING CLASS AVERAGE		
5. DIFFERENCE BETWEEN YOUR SCORE AND CLASS AVERAGE (+ or −)		
6. DIFFERENCE BETWEEN YOUR PERCENTILE AND CLASS AVERAGE (+ or −)		

READY POSITION

STARTING POSITION

21.

From Head to Toe

ARM YOURSELF

CHAIR PUSHUPS - PERCENTILE RANKING

MALES AGE									PERCENTILE RANKING	FEMALES AGE								
10	11	12	13	14	15	16	17	18		10	11	12	13	14	15	16	17	18
50	52	52	51	—	—	—	—	—	99	31	35	32	35	35	33	35	36	40
38	41	44	45	50	50	—	—	—	95	25	29	25	24	27	25	26	25	26
31	34	39	40	45	50	50	—	—	90	20	22	21	21	22	21	21	21	21
29	31	35	37	42	49	50	51	52	85	18	20	20	18	20	19	20	20	20
27	29	32	34	40	45	49	49	51	80	16	18	17	17	18	17	17	17	17
24	26	30	31	36	42	47	—	—	75	14	16	16	15	16	15	16	16	15
22	24	29	30	34	40	44	48	50	70	13	15	15	14	15	14	15	15	14
20	22	26	27	31	39	41	47	—	65	11	13	13	13	14	13	13	14	13
18	20	24	25	30	36	40	44	49	60	10	12	12	12	13	12	12	13	—
16	19	22	23	27	34	37	42	46	55	9	11	11	11	12	11	11	12	12
15	16	21	21	25	31	35	40	43	50	8	10	10	10	10	10	10	11	—
14	15	20	20	24	30	33	38	41	45	7	8	9	8	9	9	9	—	11
13	13	18	19	22	29	31	36	40	40	6	7	7	7	8	8	8	10	10
12	12	16	17	21	26	30	33	37	35	5	6	6	6	7	7	7	9	9
11	10	14	15	20	24	28	31	35	30	—	5	5	5	6	6	6	8	7
10	9	13	14	18	22	25	27	31	25	4	4	4	4	5	5	5	7	6
8	8	11	12	16	20	23	25	30	20	3	3	3	3	4	4	4	6	5
7	7	9	10	13	18	20	24	26	15	2	2	—	2	3	3	3	5	4
5	5	7	8	10	15	18	21	21	10	—	—	2	—	2	2	2	3	3
3	3	4	5	7	11	12	18	15	5	1	1	1	1	1	1	1	2	2

NUMBER OF PUSHUPS ACHIEVED

From Head to Toe

ARM YOURSELF

#	NAME	# OF PUSHUPS TRIAL 1	PERCENTILE RANKING	# OF PUSHUPS TRIAL 2	PERCENTILE RANKING
1.					
2.					
3.					
4.					
5.					
6.					
7.					
8.					
9.					
10.					
11.					
12.					
13.					
14.					
15.					
16.					
17.					
18.					
19.					
20.					
21.					
22.					
23.					
24.					
25.					
26.					
27.					
28.					
29.					
30.					
31.					
32.					
33.					
	CLASS TOTAL				
	CLASS AVERAGE				

(CLASS TOTAL ÷ NUMBER OF STUDENTS)

From Head to Toe

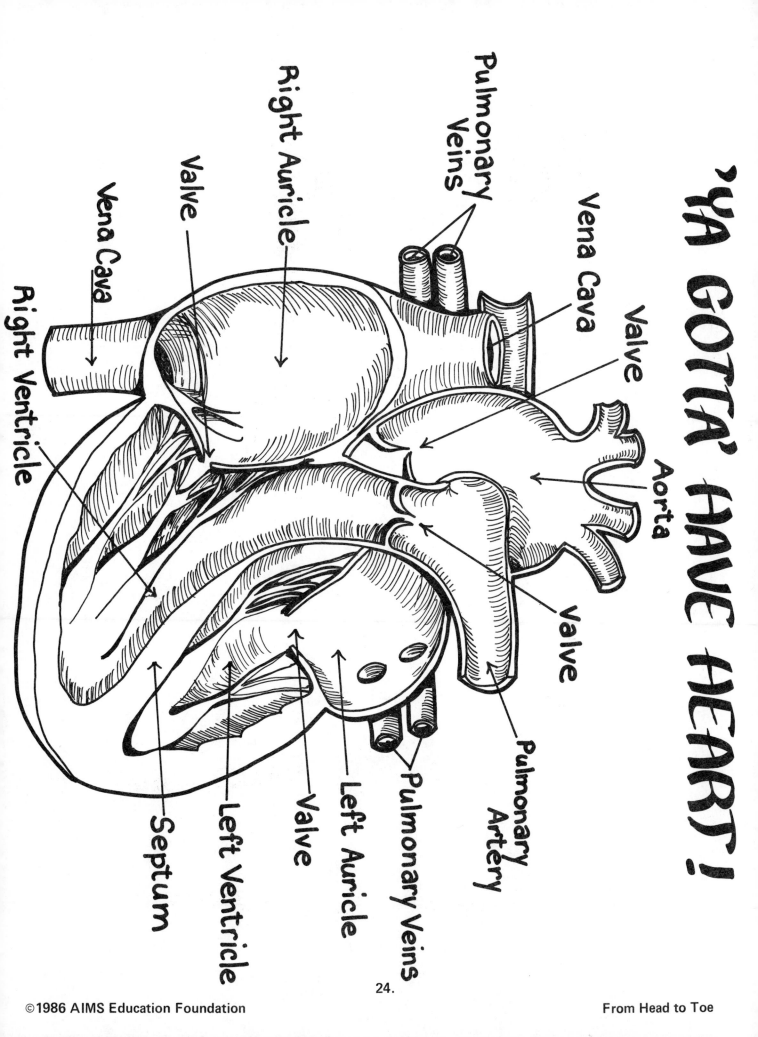

"YA GOTTA' HAVE HEART!"

Pulmonary Veins

Vena Cava

Right Auricle

Valve

Vena Cava

Right Ventricle

Valve

Aorta

Valve

Pulmonary Artery

Pulmonary Veins

Left Auricle

Valve

Left Ventricle

Septum

24.

From Head to Toe

'YA GOTTA' HAVE HEART!

CREATE YOUR OWN STETHOSCOPE

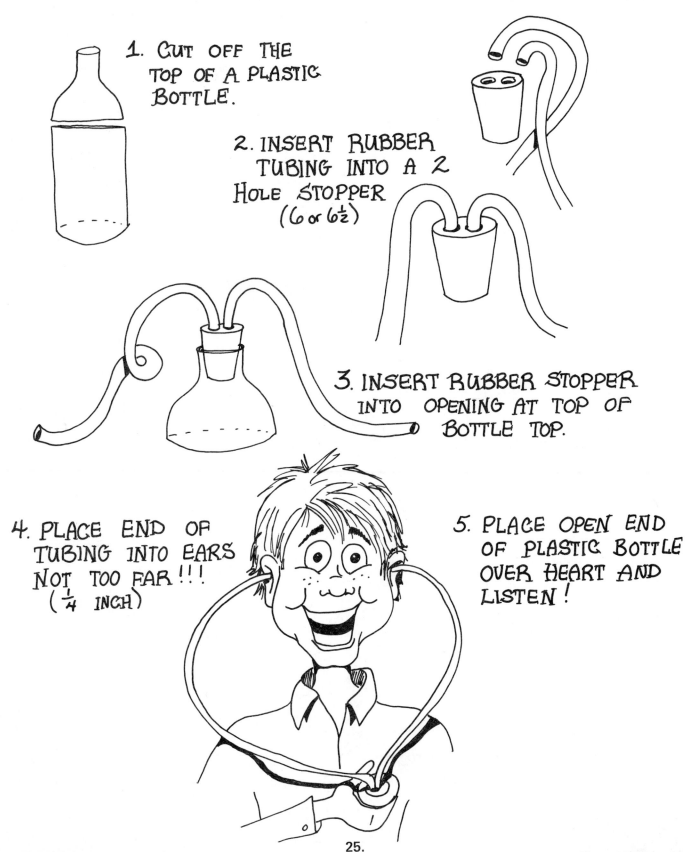

1. CUT OFF THE TOP OF A PLASTIC BOTTLE.

2. INSERT RUBBER TUBING INTO A 2 HOLE STOPPER (6 or 6½)

3. INSERT RUBBER STOPPER INTO OPENING AT TOP OF BOTTLE TOP.

4. PLACE END OF TUBING INTO EARS NOT TOO FAR!!! (¼ INCH)

5. PLACE OPEN END OF PLASTIC BOTTLE OVER HEART AND LISTEN!

25.

From Head to Toe

"YA GOTTA' HAVE HEART!"

SURFACE AREA OF THE HEART

TRY TO DO THE HEART'S WORK

THE HEART IS A MOST POWERFUL MUSCLE. TO GET A GRASP ON HOW HARD IT WORKS FOR YOU — TRY THIS EXPERIMENT. TAKE A TENNIS BALL IN YOUR HAND. THE FORCE NEEDED TO SQUEEZE THE TENNIS BALL IS SIMILAR TO THE FORCE NEEDED TO SQUEEZE THE BLOOD OUT OF YOUR HEART. SQUEEZE THE BALL 10 TIMES. NOW, SQUEEZE IT 60 TIMES A MINUTE. YOU NOW HAVE AN IDEA OF HOW HARD YOUR HEART WORKS!

NEXT: IT IS POSSIBLE TO CALCULATE YOUR OWN HEART'S STROKE VOLUME – (THE AMOUNT OF BLOOD PUMPED IN ONE BEAT OF YOUR HEART). USE THE SURFACE AREA OF THE HEART CHART AT THE RIGHT. FIND YOUR HEIGHT; THE SURFACE AREA OF YOUR HEART IS BESIDE YOUR HEIGHT IN THE CHART. RECORD BELOW. NOW, MULTIPLY YOUR SURFACE AREA X 3.1 TO GET YOUR CARDIAC OUTPUT. TAKE YOUR CARDIAC OUTPUT AND DIVIDE IT BY YOUR PULSE RATE AT REST. THIS IS YOUR STROKE VOLUME OR HOW MUCH BLOOD YOUR HEART PUMPS IN ONE BEAT!

SURFACE AREA OF THE HEART	
HEIGHT	SURFACE AREA in dm²
4'1'	1.25
4'2"	1.30
4'3"	1.35
4'4"	1.4
4'5"	1.43
4'6"	1.45
4'7"	1.5
4'8"	1.55
4'9"	1.6
4'10"	1.65
4'11"	1.68
5'	1.7
5'1"	1.75
5'2"	1.8
5'3"	1.85
5'4"	1.9
5'5"	1.93
5'6"	1.95
5'7"	2.0
5'8"	2.05
5'9"	2.1
5'10"	2.15
5'11"	2.18
6'	2.2

HEIGHT [ ]

(SQUARE DECIMETERS)
SURFACE AREA X 3.1 = CARDIAC OUTPUT

[ ] X 3.1 = [ ]

NORMAL
CARDIAC OUTPUT ÷ PULSE RATE = STROKE VOLUME

[ ] ÷ [ ] = [ ] (LITERS OF BLOOD)
STROKE VOLUME

WHILE AT REST — HOW MANY LITERS OF BLOOD DOES YOUR HEART PUMP IN _____ 1 MINUTE _____ 1 HOUR _____ 1 DAY ?

26.

From Head to Toe

HOW DOES YOUR HEART RATE?

SIT QUIETLY FOR 3 MINUTES. TAKE YOUR PULSE AND RECORD. DO THESE EXERCISES FOR 1 MINUTE -TAKE YOUR PULSE FOR 10 SECONDS AND RECORD.

	PULSE RATE FOR 10 SECONDS	X 6 =	PULSE RATE FOR 1 MINUTE
SITTING	_____		_____
WALKING IN PLACE	_____		_____
JUMPING JACKS	_____		_____
CHAIR STEPS	_____		_____

GRAPH YOUR RESULTS:

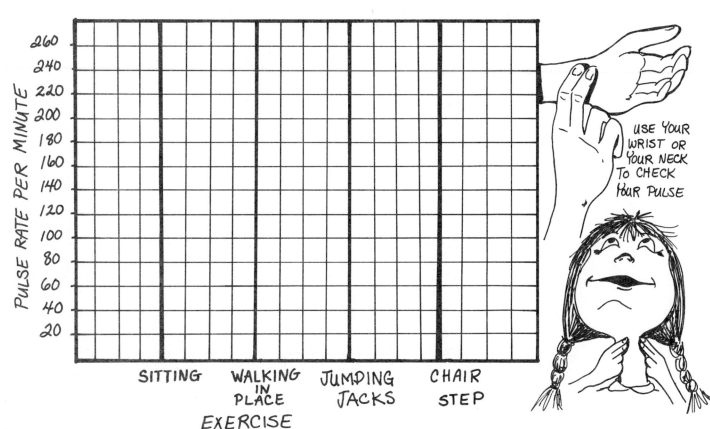

PULSE RATE PER MINUTE

260 240 220 200 180 160 140 120 100 80 60 40 20

SITTING   WALKING IN PLACE   JUMPING JACKS   CHAIR STEP

EXERCISE

USE YOUR WRIST OR YOUR NECK TO CHECK YOUR PULSE

27.

From Head to Toe

How Does Your Heart Rate?

_____ Name

Pulse Rate — Stroke Volume

Take your pulse rate for <u>10</u> seconds after each of these exercises. Multiply by six (6) to find your pulse rate for <u>1</u> minute. Next, multiply your heart rate per minute X your stroke volume to find the liters of blood per minute your heart is pumping.

	Pulse Rate (x6) 10 seconds	Pulse Rate (X) 1 minute	stroke (=) Volume	Liters of Blood per Min.
At Rest				
Walking for 1 minute				
Running in place for 1 minute				
Jumping Jacks for 1 minute				
Sit-ups for 1 minute				
Jumping Rope for 1 minute				
1 50 meter Dash				
4-50 meter Dashes				

The heart pumps about 5 liters of blood per minute at rest!

28.

page 1

From Head to Toe

How Does Your Heart Rate?

Breath Rate - Lung Capacity

Since you will be counting your pulse rate, you will need a partner to count your breath rate. After each exercise, your partner will count how many breaths you take in 10 seconds. Record on the chart below. Multiply that number X 6 to get your breath rate per minute. Next, multiply your breath rate per minute X your lung capacity to find how many liters of air per minute you are breathing.

	Breath Rate 10 seconds	Breath Rate 1 minute	(X) Lung Capacity	(=) Liters of Air per Minute
At Rest				
Walking for 1 minute				
Running in place for 1 minute				
Jumping Jacks for 1 minute				
Sit-ups for 1 minute				
Jumping Rope for 1 minute				
1 50 meter Dash				
4- 50 meter Dashes				

You've got a lot of hot air!

29.

page 2

From Head to Toe

How Does Your Heart Rate?

PULSE RATE AFTER EXERCISE

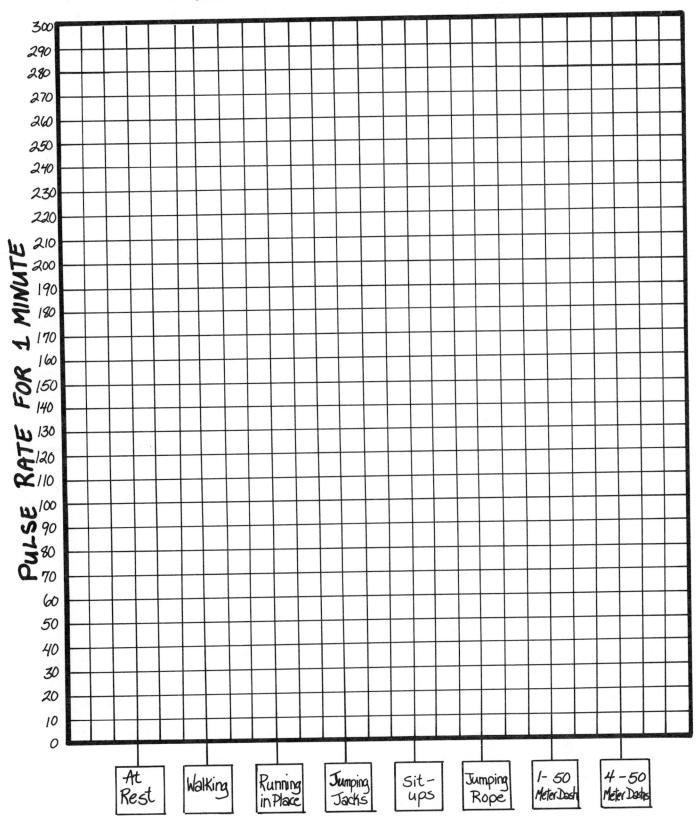

At Rest | Walking | Running in Place | Jumping Jacks | Sit-ups | Jumping Rope | 1-50 Meter Dash | 4-50 Meter Dashes

EXERCISES

Pulse Rate for 1 Minute

30.

From Head to Toe

How Does Your Heart Rate?

LITERS OF BLOOD PUMPED BY THE HEART

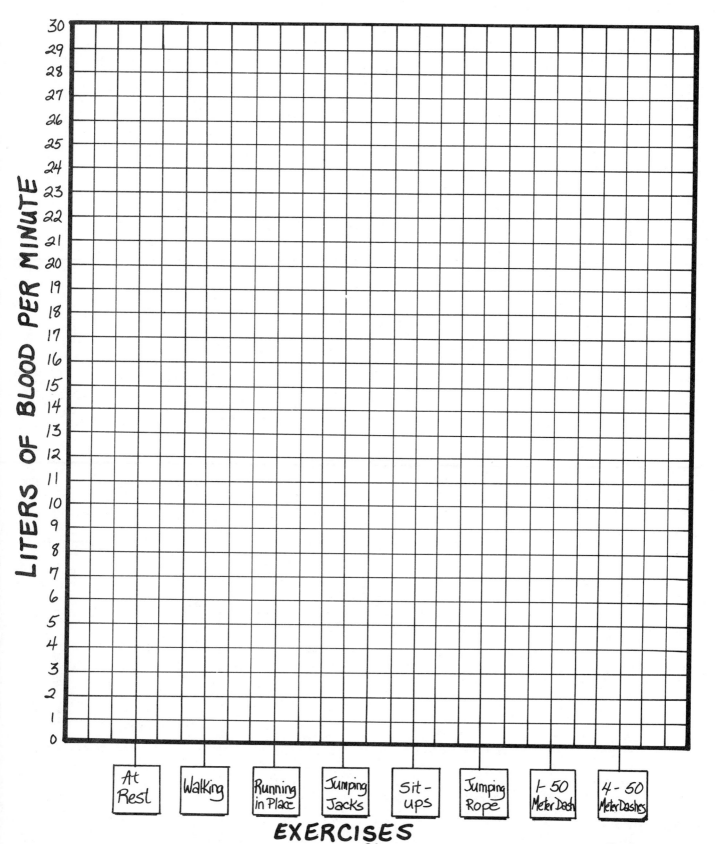

_____ Name

LITERS OF BLOOD PER MINUTE

30
29
28
27
26
25
24
23
22
21
20
19
18
17
16
15
14
13
12
11
10
9
8
7
6
5
4
3
2
1
0

At Rest | Walking | Running in Place | Jumping Jacks | Sit-ups | Jumping Rope | 1-50 Meter Dash | 4-50 Meter Dashes

EXERCISES

31.

From Head to Toe

How Does Your Heart Rate?

BREATH RATE AFTER EXERCISE

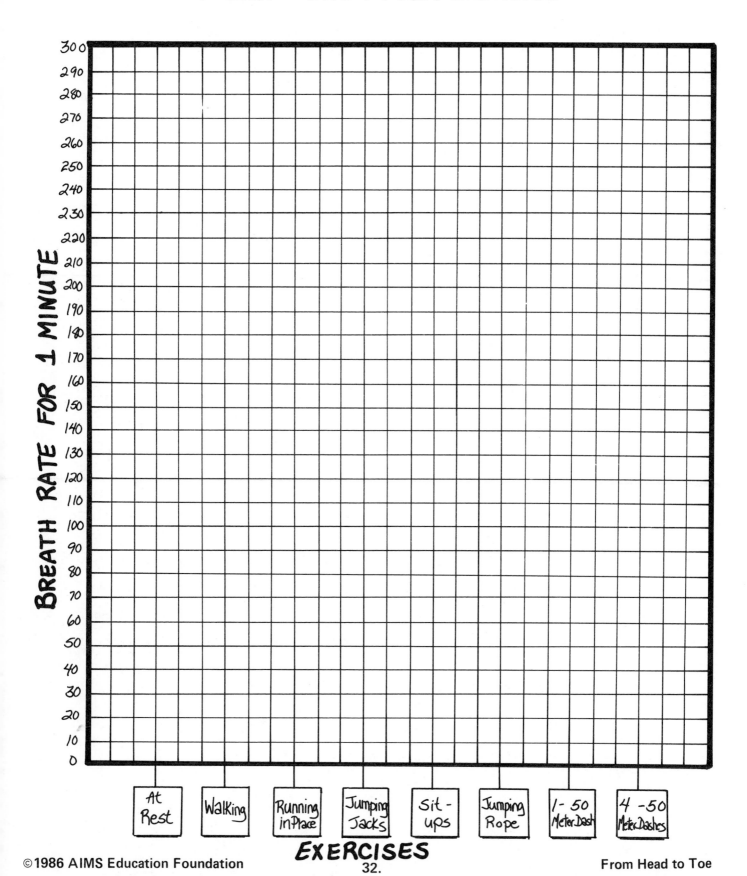

32.

From Head to Toe

How Does Your Heart Rate?

LITERS OF AIR BREATHED

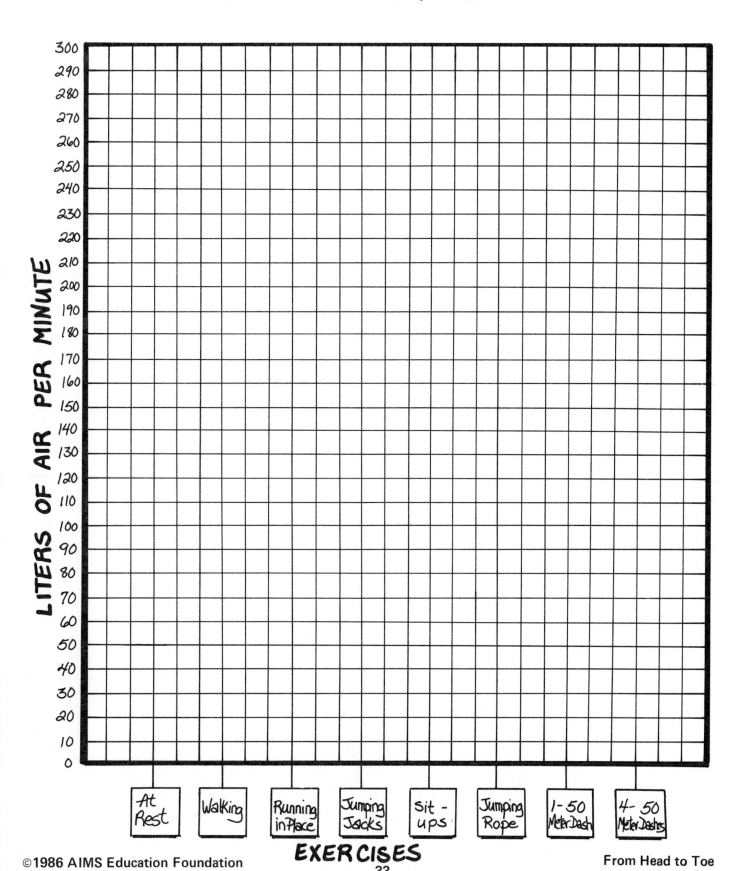

LITERS OF AIR PER MINUTE

300
290
280
270
260
250
240
230
220
210
200
190
180
170
160
150
140
130
120
110
100
90
80
70
60
50
40
30
20
10
0

| At Rest | Walking | Running in Place | Jumping Jacks | Sit-ups | Jumping Rope | 1-50 Meter Dash | 4-50 Meter Dashes |

EXERCISES

33.

From Head to Toe

The Pressure's On

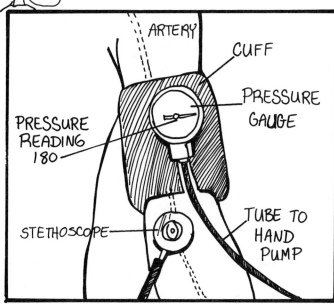

Squeeze the hand pump of the blood pressure cuff until the pressure gauge reads 180. The arterial blood flow is now momentarily blocked.

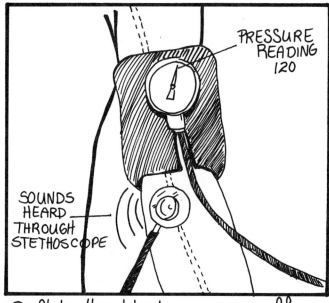

Deflate the blood pressure cuff until you hear the blood begin to squirt through the artery. Whatever pressure reading appears at this point is the systolic blood pressure.

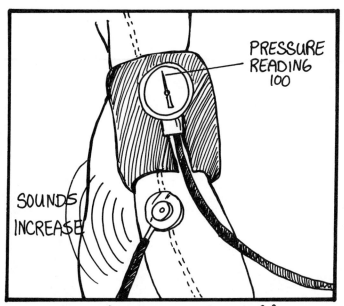

As you decrease the cuff pressure, sounds in the stethoscope will increase as more blood rushes through the artery.

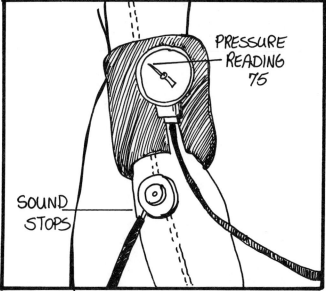

When the cuff pressure decreases enough to let the blood flow freely, all sounds in the stethoscope stop. The pressure reading at the moment the sound stops is the diastolic blood pressure.

From Head to Toe

The Pressure's On

NORMAL BLOOD PRESSURE

SIT QUIETLY FOR 5 MINUTES. TAKE YOUR BLOOD PRESSURE TWICE. RECORD. FIND THE AVERAGE.

BLOOD PRESSURE

	SYSTOLIC		DIASTOLIC
TRIAL #1	_____	/	_____
TRIAL #2	_____	/	_____
TOTAL	_____	/	_____
AVERAGE	_____	/	_____

BLOOD PRESSURE AFTER EXERCISE

PICK AN EXERCISE: RUN OR WALK 440, RUN OR WALK IN PLACE, DO CHAIR PUSHUPS. AFTERWARDS – TAKE YOUR BLOOD PRESSURE TWICE – AVERAGE.

BLOOD PRESSURE

	SYSTOLIC		DIASTOLIC
TRIAL #1	_____	/	_____
TRIAL #2	_____	/	_____
TOTAL	_____	/	_____
AVERAGE	_____	/	_____

TAKE YOUR AVERAGE NORMAL BLOOD PRESSURE AND YOUR AVERAGE PRESSURE AFTER EXERCISE AND COMPARE THEM.

BLOOD PRESSURE

	SYSTOLIC		DIASTOLIC
NORMAL	_____	/	_____
AFTER EXERCISE	_____	/	_____
DIFFERENCE	_____	/	_____

From Head to Toe

The Pressure's On
MASTER AVERAGE SHEET

SYSTOLIC
DIASTOLIC

BLOOD PRESSURE
SYSTOLIC / DIASTOLIC

#	NAME	SYSTOLIC / DIASTOLIC
1.		/
2.		/
3.		/
4.		/
5.		/
6.		/
7.		/
8.		/
9.		/
10.		/
11.		/
12.		/
13.		/
14.		/
15.		/
16.		/
17.		/
18.		/
19.		/
20.		/
21.		/
22.		/
23.		/
24.		/
25.		/
26.		/
27.		/
28.		/
29.		/
30.		/
31.		/
32.		/
33.		/
CLASS TOTAL		/
CLASS AVERAGE		/

From Head to Toe

Step In Time

Name _____

How Fast Does Your Heart Return To Its Resting Rate After Different Activities?

Lie Flat on Back

Sit in chair (Resting Rate)

Sit then stand up

Walk in Place

Run in Place

Run 50 Meters

PULSE RATE (For 10 Seconds) x6 (For 1 Minute)		Recovery Time
		0 sec.
		0 sec.
		sec.
		sec.
		sec.
		sec.

After You Record All Your Data, Make a Line Graph to Show Your Recovery Time

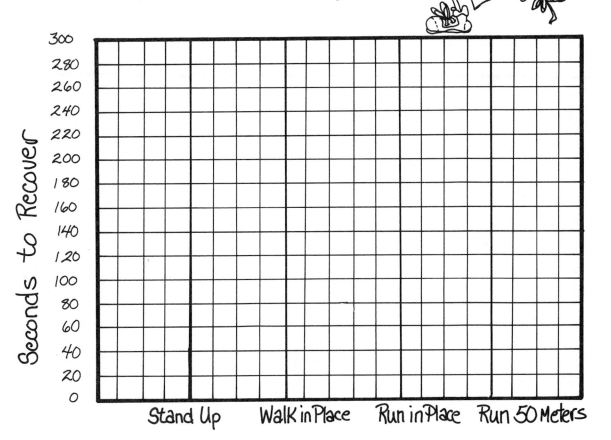

Seconds to Recover

300
280
260
240
220
200
180
160
140
120
100
80
60
40
20
0

Stand Up   Walk in Place   Run in Place   Run 50 Meters

From Head to Toe

Step In Time

—————————— name

STANDING

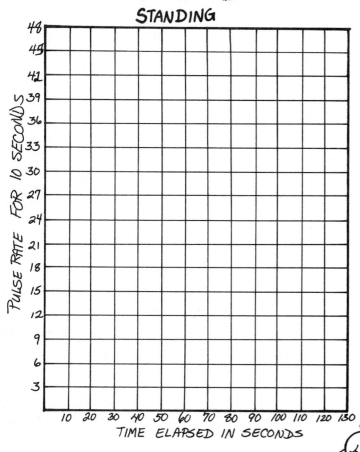

Y-axis: PULSE RATE FOR 10 SECONDS — 3, 6, 9, 12, 15, 18, 21, 24, 27, 30, 33, 36, 39, 42, 45, 48

X-axis: 10 20 30 40 50 60 70 80 90 100 110 120 130

TIME ELAPSED IN SECONDS

WALKING IN PLACE

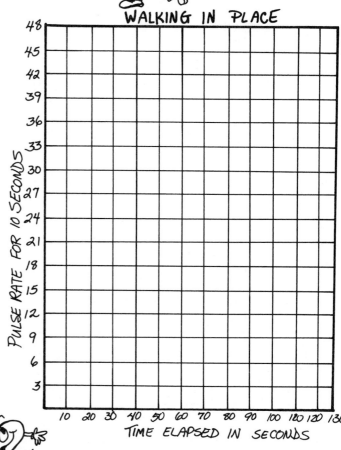

Y-axis: PULSE RATE FOR 10 SECONDS — 3, 6, 9, 12, 15, 18, 21, 24, 27, 30, 33, 36, 39, 42, 45, 48

X-axis: 10 20 30 40 50 60 70 80 90 100 110 120 130

TIME ELAPSED IN SECONDS

RUNNING IN PLACE

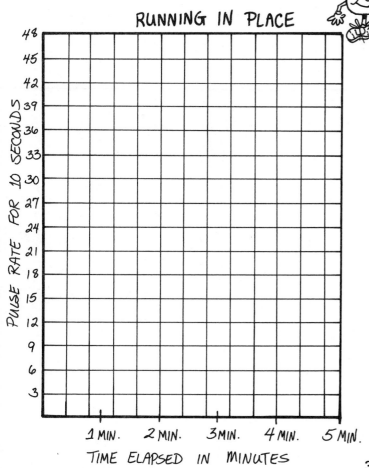

Y-axis: PULSE RATE FOR 10 SECONDS — 3, 6, 9, 12, 15, 18, 21, 24, 27, 30, 33, 36, 39, 42, 45, 48

X-axis: 1 MIN. 2 MIN. 3 MIN. 4 MIN. 5 MIN.

TIME ELAPSED IN MINUTES

RUNNING 50 METERS

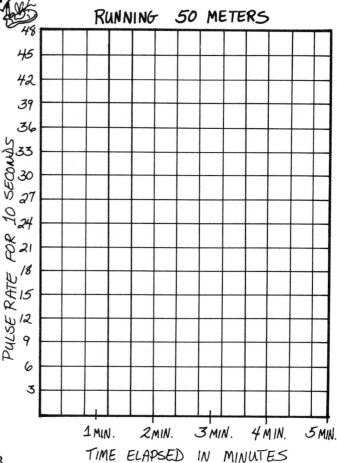

Y-axis: PULSE RATE FOR 10 SECONDS — 3, 6, 9, 12, 15, 18, 21, 24, 27, 30, 33, 36, 39, 42, 45, 48

X-axis: 1 MIN. 2 MIN. 3 MIN. 4 MIN. 5 MIN.

TIME ELAPSED IN MINUTES

38.

From Head to Toe

Temperature's Rising!
Personal Temperature Cycle
for :

Take Your Temperature every 2 Hours and Record.

7:00 AM. _____

9:00 A.M. _____

11:00 A.M. _____

1:00 P.M. _____

3:00 P.M. _____

5:00 P.M. _____

7:00 P.M. _____

9:00 P.M. _____

TOTAL _____

AVERAGE _____

What time was your temperature highest? _____

What time was your temperature lowest? _____

How does your average temperature compare with normal 98.6°? _____

_____

39.

From Head to Toe

Name_____

Temperature's Rising!

Group Recording Sheet

Group Name _____

Exercise _____

Name	Preactivity Temperature	Postactivity Temperature	Difference + or −
1.			
2.			
3.			
4.			
5.			
6.			
Totals			
Averages			

From Head to Toe

AM I YOUR TYPE?

1. STERILIZE TIP OF INDEX FINGER WITH ALCOHOL PAD. ALLOW TO AIR DRY.
2. APPLY FORCE WITH YOUR THUMB TO THE BASE OF FIRST JOINT OF INDEX FINGER.
3. TAKE THE LANCET BETWEEN YOUR INDEX FINGER AND THE THUMB OF YOUR WORKING HAND. LINE UP TIP WITH THE PAD OF THE INDEX FINGER. WITH A SHORT FORCEFUL JAB, POKE ONE HOLE IN TIP OF INDEX FINGER.

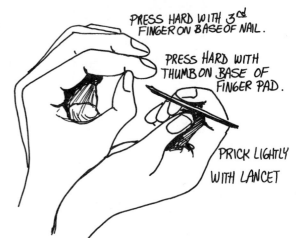

PRESS HARD WITH 3rd FINGER ON BASE OF NAIL.

PRESS HARD WITH THUMB ON BASE OF FINGER PAD.

PRICK LIGHTLY WITH LANCET

4. BLOT FIRST DROP OF BLOOD ON ALCOHOL PAD. PLACE LANCET ON PAPER TOWEL FOR LATER DISPOSAL. USING YOUR THUMB, SQUEEZE ONE DROP OF BLOOD FROM FINGERTIP - PLACE DROP IN CIRCLE A. PLACE A SECOND DROP IN CIRCLE B. RAISE YOUR HAND TO RECEIVE ANTI-GLUTENS. (PLACE ALCOHOL PAD ON PUNCTURE AND HOLD IN PLACE WITH YOUR THUMB.)

5. AFTER RECEIVING ANTI-A AND ANTI-B SOLUTIONS, STIR ANTI-A CIRCLE THOROUGHLY WITH SIDE OF TOOTHPICK. BE SURE TO SPREAD MIXTURE OUT TO FILL ENTIRE CIRCLE. DISCARD TOOTHPICK ON PAPER TOWEL. GET A SECOND TOOTHPICK AND REPEAT OPERATION FOR ANTI-B CIRCLE. DISCARD TOOTHPICK ONTO PAPER TOWEL.

6. PICK UP HEMO-CARD AND GENTLY ROCK FOR ABOUT ONE/TWO MINUTES. SET CARD DOWN AND WATCH RESULTS. RECORD YOUR BLOOD TYPE.

I HAVE BLOOD TYPE _____.

IF A & B REMAIN THE SAME - YOU HAVE BLOOD TYPE O.

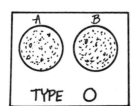

TYPE O

IF CIRCLE A SHOWS CLOTTING AND B DOESN'T, YOU ARE TYPE A.

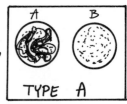

TYPE A

IF CIRCLE B CLOTS AND A REMAINS UNCHANGED, YOU HAVE TYPE B.

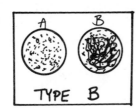

TYPE B

IF BOTH CIRCLE A AND B CLOT, YOU HAVE AB BLOOD.

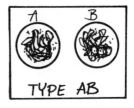

TYPE AB

41.

From Head to Toe

AM I YOUR TYPE?
Ingredients in Blood

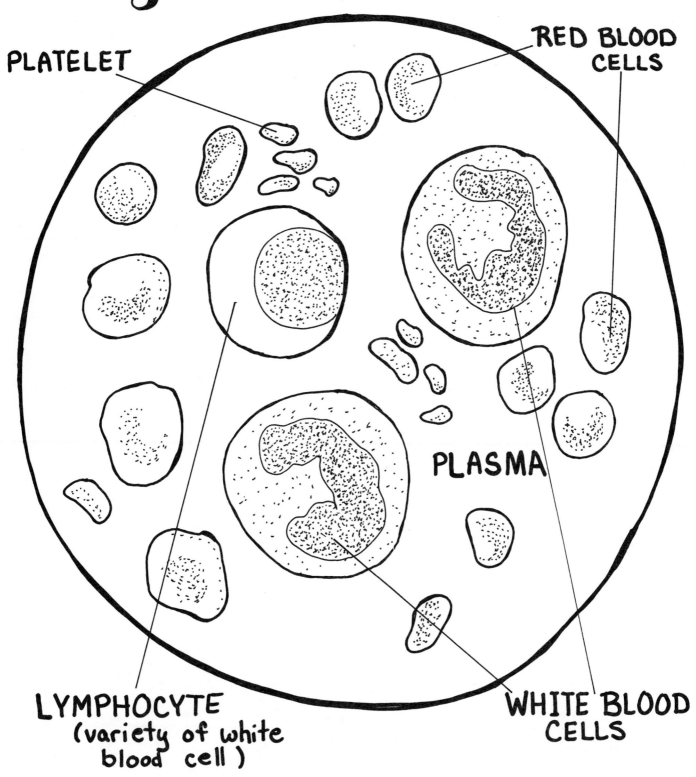

PLATELET

RED BLOOD CELLS

PLASMA

LYMPHOCYTE
(variety of white blood cell)

WHITE BLOOD CELLS

From Head to Toe

AM I YOUR TYPE?

NAMES	BLOOD TYPE			
	A	B	O	A/B
1.				
2.				
3.				
4.				
5.				
6.				
7.				
8.				
9.				
10.				
11.				
12.				
13.				
14.				
15.				
16.				
17.	A	B	O	A/B

NAMES	BLOOD TYPE			
	A	B	O	A/B
18.				
19.				
20.				
21.				
22.				
23.				
24.				
25.				
26.				
27.				
28.				
29.				
30.				
31.				
32.				
33.				
34.	A	B	O	A/B

43.

From Head to Toe

Take A Breather!

PERSONAL LUNG CAPACITY

1. Blow up a balloon (sphere).
2. Measure its circumference (C) in cm.
3. Record
4. Find the volume
5. Make 4 trials
6. Find the average

The volume of a sphere can be calculated by the formula $V = \frac{4}{3}\pi r^3$

LUNG CAPACITY

TRIAL #	CIRCUMFERENCE C	$C \div \pi(3.14) =$ DIAMETER (d)	$d \div 2 =$ RADIUS (r)	$r^3 =$ $r \times r \times r \times \pi(3.14) \times \frac{4}{3} =$	VOLUME cm³	liters
1	cm	$\frac{C=\underline{\quad}}{3.14} = d$	$\frac{d=\underline{\quad}}{2} = r$	$r^3 = \underline{\quad} \times \pi = \underline{\quad} \times \frac{4}{3} =$		
2	cm	$\frac{C=\underline{\quad}}{3.14} = d$	$\frac{d=\underline{\quad}}{2} = r$	$r^3 = \underline{\quad} \times \pi = \underline{\quad} \times \frac{4}{3} =$		
3	cm	$\frac{C=\underline{\quad}}{3.14} = d$	$\frac{d=\underline{\quad}}{2} = r$	$r^3 = \underline{\quad} \times \pi = \underline{\quad} \times \frac{4}{3} =$		
4	cm	$\frac{C=\underline{\quad}}{3.14} = d$	$\frac{d=\underline{\quad}}{2} = r$	$r^3 = \underline{\quad} \times \pi = \underline{\quad} \times \frac{4}{3} =$		

Total

Average

NAME _____

44.

From Head to Toe

Take A Breather!
INTERVIEW SHEET

NAME _____
DATE _____
SEX _____
AGE _____
HEIGHT_____
WEIGHT_____
MINUTES OF STRENUOUS
EXERCISE PER DAY _____
SMOKING HABITS
OF PACKS PER DAY _____

LUNG CAPACITY

AFTER YOU BREATHE OUT NORMALLY, BLOW THE REST (RESERVE) OF YOUR AIR INTO THE BALLOON. MEASURE THE CIRCUMFERENCE AND RECORD

TAKE THE DEEPEST BREATH YOU CAN.... BLOW EVERY BIT OF YOUR AIR INTO THE BALLOON. MEASURE THE CIRCUMFERENCE AND RECORD.

RESERVE AIR CAPACITY

TRIAL #1	
TRIAL #2	
TRIAL #3	
TOTAL	
AVERAGE	

VITAL CAPACITY

TRIAL #1	
TRIAL #2	
TRIAL #3	
TOTAL	
AVERAGE	

45.

From Head to Toe

TAKE A BREATHER
(Factors Affecting Lung Capacity)

VITAL AIR VOLUME ☐ COLOR   RESERVE AIR VOLUME ☐ COLOR

AGE IN YEARS

CIRCUMFERENCE OF BALLOON IN CM	MALES	FEMALES	0-5	6-10	11-15	16-20	21-30	31-40	41-50	51-60	60-70	>70
120												
100												
90												
80												
70												
60												
50												
40												
30												
20												
10												

HEIGHT IN CM

100	110	120	130	140	150	160	170	180	190	200

MASTER DATA SHEET

WEIGHT IN POUNDS

CIRCUMFERENCE OF BALLOON IN CM	BELOW 50	51-75	76-100	100-125	126-150	151-175	176-200	>200
120								
100								
90								
80								
70								
60								
50								
40								
30								
20								
10								

MINUTES OF EXERCISE

<20	20	30	40	50	60	70	80	90	100	>100

SMOKING HABITS - # OF PACKS PER DAY

NON SMOKER	<½	½-1	1-2	2-3	>3

46.

From Head to Toe

Take A Breather!

BREATHING

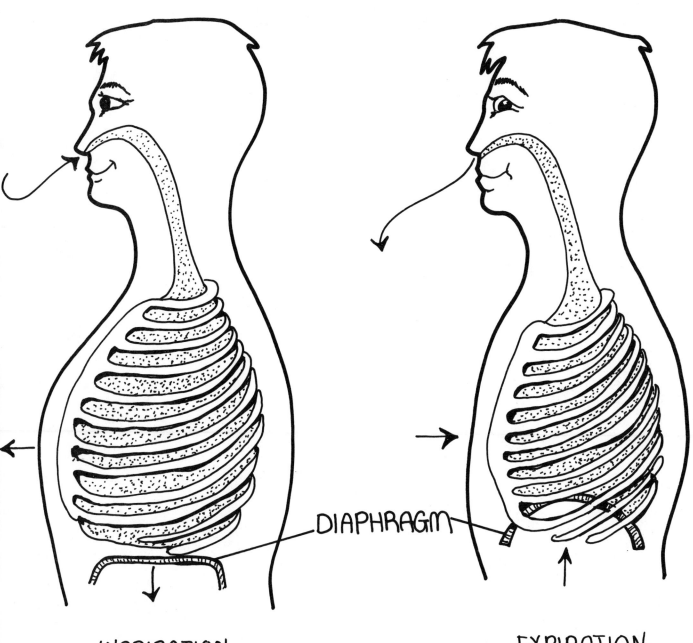

INSPIRATION   EXPIRATION

From Head to Toe

Take A Breather!

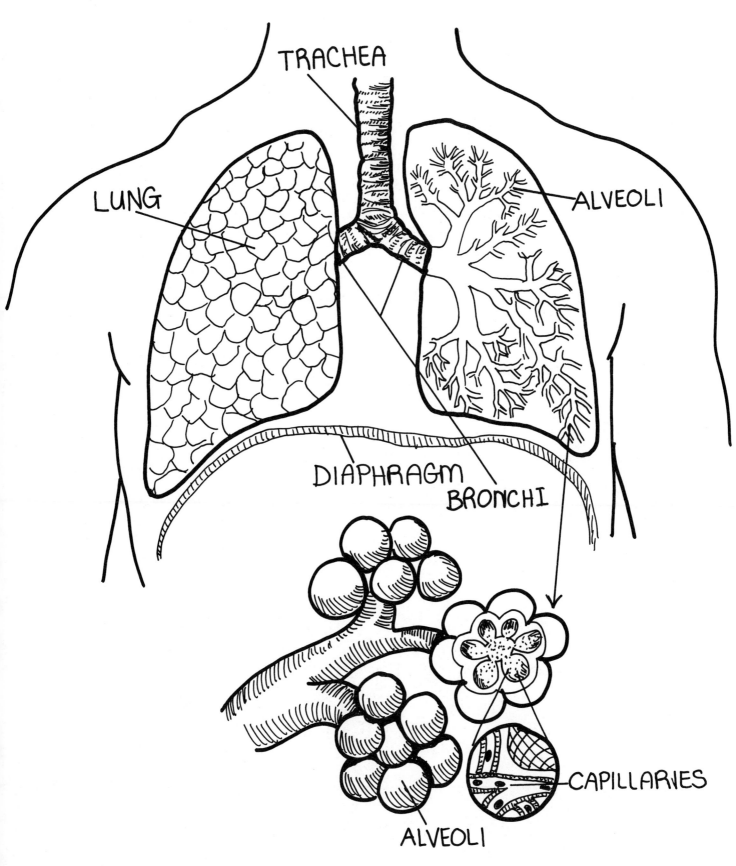

TRACHEA

LUNG

ALVEOLI

DIAPHRAGM

BRONCHI

ALVEOLI

CAPILLARIES

48.

From Head to Toe

_____ name.

You Take My Breath Away

Data Table for Number of Breaths per Minute

	Estimate	Trial 1	Trial 2	Trial 3	Average
Sitting					
Jogging					
Cycling					

First: Estimate how many breaths per minute you think you will take for each activity. Record. Next, do the activities, count your breaths for 3 trials. Average. Now, compare your breath rates by graphing.

Sitting

Jogging

Cycling

4 8 12 16 20 24 28 32 36 40 44 48 52 56 60 64 68 72 76 80 84 88 92 96 100

Number of Breaths per Minute

49.

From Head to Toe

CLASS AVERAGE

	Name	
1.		
2.		
3.		
4.		
5.		
6.		
7.		
8.		
9.		
10.		
11.		
12.		
13.		
14.		
15.		
16.		
17.		
18.		
19.		
20.		
21.		
22.		
23.		
24.		
25.		
26.		
27.		
28.		
29.		
30.		
31.		
32.		
33.		
34.		
35.		

CLASS TOTAL
50. CLASS AVERAGE

The AIMS Program

AIMS is the acronym for "Activities Integrating Mathematics and Science." Such integration enriches learning and makes it meaningful and holistic. AIMS began as a project of Fresno Pacific College to integrate the study of mathematics and science in Grades K-9, but has since expanded to include language arts, social studies, and other disciplines.

AIMS is a continuing program of the non-profit AIMS Education Foundation. It had its inception in a National Science Foundation funded program whose purpose was to explore the effectiveness of integrating mathematics and science. The project directors in cooperation with eighty elementary classroom teachers devoted two years to a thorough field-testing of the results and implications of integration.

The approach met with such positive results that the decision was made to launch a program to create instructional materials incorporating this concept. Despite the fact that thoughtful educators have long recommended an integrative approach, very little appropriate material was available in 1981 when the project began. A series of writing projects have ensued and today the AIMS Education Foundation is committed to continue the creation of new integrated activities on a permanent basis.

The AIMS program is funded through the sale of this developing series of books and proceeds from the Foundation's endowment. All net income from book and poster sales flow into a trust fund administered by the AIMS Education Foundation. Use of these funds is restricted to support of research, development, publication of new materials, and partial scholarships for classroom teachers participating in writing and field testing teams. Writers donate all their rights to the Foundation to support its on-going program. No royalties are paid to the writers.

The rationale for integration lies in the fact that science, mathematics, language arts, social studies, etc., are integrally interwoven in the real world from which it follows that they should be similarly treated in the classroom where we are preparing students to live in that world. Teachers who use the AIMS program give enthusiastic endorsement to the effectiveness of this approach.

Science encompasses the art of questioning, investigating, hypothesizing, discovering and communicating. Mathematics is the language that provides clarity, objectivity, and understanding. The language arts provide us powerful tools of communication. Many of the major contemporary societal issues stem from advancements in science and must be studied in the context of the social sciences. Therefore, it is timely that all of us take seriously a more holistic mode of educating our students. This goal motivates all who are associated with the AIMS Program. We invite you to join us in this effort.

Meaningful integration of knowledge is a major recommendation coming from the nation's professional science and mathematics associations. The American Association for the Advancement of Science in *Science for All Americans* strongly recommends the integration of mathematics, science and technology. The National Council of Teachers of Mathematics places strong emphasis on applications of mathematics such as are found in science investigations. AIMS is fully aligned with these recommendations.

Extensive field testing of AIMS investigations confirms these beneficial results.

1. Mathematics becomes more meaningful, hence more useful, when it is applied to situations that interest students.
2. The extent to which science is studied and understood is increased, with a significant economy of time, when mathematics and science are integrated.
3. There is improved quality of learning and retention, supporting the thesis that learning which is meaningful and relevant is more effective.
4. Motivation and involvement are increased dramatically as students investigate real world situations and participate actively in the process.

We invite you to become part of this classroom teacher movement by using an integrated approach to learning and sharing any suggestions you may have. The AIMS Program welcomes you!

AIMS Education Foundation Programs

A Day With AIMS

Intensive one-day workshops are offered to introduce educators to the philosophy and rationale of AIMS. Participants will discuss the methodology of AIMS and the strategies by which AIMS principles may be incorporated into curriculum. Each participant will take part in a variety of hands-on AIMS investigations to gain an understanding of such aspects as the scientific/mathematical content, classroom management, and connections with other curricular areas. The *A Day With AIMS* workshops may be offered anywhere in the United States. Necessary supplies and take-home materials are usually included in the enrollment fee.

AIMS One-Week Off-Campus Workshops

Throughout the nation, AIMS offers many one-week workshops each year, usually in the summer. Each workshop lasts five days and includes at least 30 hours of AIMS hands-on instruction. Participants are grouped according to the grade level(s) in which they are interested. Instructors are members of the AIMS National Leadership Network. Supplies for the activities and a generous supply of take-home materials are included in the enrollment fee. Sites are selected on the basis of applications submitted by educational organizations. If chosen to host a workshop, the host agency agrees to provide specified facilities and cooperate in the promotion of the workshop. The AIMS Education Foundation supplies workshop materials as well as the travel, housing, and meals for instructors.

AIMS One-Week On-Campus Workshops

Each summer, Fresno Pacific College offers AIMS one-week workshops on the campus of Fresno Pacific College in Fresno, California. AIMS Program Directors and highly qualified members of the AIMS National Leadership Network serve as instructors.

The Science Festival and the Festival of Mathematics

Each summer, Fresno Pacific College offers a Science Festival and a Festival of Mathematics. These two-week festivals have gained national recognition as inspiring and challenging experiences, giving unique opportunities to experience hands-on mathematics and science in topical and grade level groups. Guest faculty includes some of the nation's most highly regarded mathematics and science educators. Supplies and take-home materials are included in the enrollment fee.

The AIMS National Leadership Program

This is an AIMS staff development program seeking to prepare facilitators for a leadership roles in science/math education in their home districts or regions. Upon successful completion of the program, trained facilitators become members of the AIMS National Leadership Network, qualified to conduct AIMS workshops, teach AIMS in-service courses for college credit, and serve as AIMS consultants. Intensive training is provided in mathematics, science, processing skills, workshop management, and other relevant topics.

College Credit and Grants

Those who participate in workshops may often qualify for college credit. If the workshop takes place on the campus of Fresno Pacific College, that institution may grant appropriate credit. If the workshop takes place off-campus, arrangements can sometimes be made for credit to be granted by another college or university. In addition, the applicant's home school district is often willing to grant in-service or professional development credit. Many educators who participate in AIMS workshops are recipients of various types of educational grants, either local or national. Nationally known foundations and funding agencies have long recognized the value of AIMS mathematics and science workshops to educators. The AIMS Education Foundation encourages educators interested in attending or hosting workshops to explore the possibilities suggested above. Although the Foundation strongly supports such interest, it reminds applicants that they have the primary responsibility for fulfilling *current* requirements.

For current information regarding the programs described above, please complete the following:

AIMS Program Publications

GRADES 5-9 SERIES

Math + Science, A Solution
The Sky's the Limit
From Head to Toe
Fun With Foods
Floaters and Sinkers
Down to Earth
Our Wonderful World
Pieces and Patterns, A Patchwork in Math and Science
Piezas y Diseños, un Mosaic de Matemáticas y Ciencias
Out of This World
Soap Films and Bubbles
Finding Your Bearings
Electrical Connections
Historical Connections in Mathematics

GRADES K-4 SERIES

Fall Into Math and Science
Cáete de Gusto Hacia el Otoño con la Matemáticas y Ciencias
Glide Into Winter With Math and Science
Patine al Invierno con Matemáticas y Ciencias
Spring Into Math and Science
Brinca de Alegria Hacia la Primavera con las Matemáticas y Ciencias
Seasoning Math and Science, Book A (Fall and Winter)
Seasoning Math and Science, Book B (Spring and Summer)
Jawbreakers and Heart Thumpers
Hardhatting in a Geo-World
Popping With Power
Overhead and Underfoot
Primarily Plants
Primariamente Plantas
Primarily Physics
Primariamente Física

GRADES K-6 SERIES

Primarily Bears
Ositos Nada Más
Water Precious Water
Critters
Mostly Magnets

FOR FURTHER INFORMATION WRITE TO:

AIMS Education Foundation • P.O. Box 8120 • Fresno, California 93747-8120

We invite you to subscribe to the
AIMS Newsletter!

Each issue of the AIMS Newsletter contains a variety of material useful to educators at all grade levels. Feature articles of lasting value deal with topics such as mathematical or science concepts, curriculum, assessment, the teaching of processing skills, and historical background. Several of the latest AIMS math/science investigations are always included, along with their reproducible activity sheets. As needs direct and space allows, various issues contain news of current developments, such as workshop schedules, activities of the AIMS National Leadership Network, and announcements of upcoming publications.

The AIMS Newsletter is published monthly, August through May. Subscriptions are on an annual basis only. A subscription entered at any time will begin with the next issue, but will also include the previous issues of that year or volume. Readers have preferred this arrangement because articles and activities within an annual volume are often interrelated.

Please note that an AIMS Newsletter subscription automatically includes duplication rights for one school site for all issues of the Newsletter included in the subscription. Many schools build cost-effective library resources with their subscriptions.

YES! I am interested in receiving the AIMS Newsletter.

Please send the following volumes, subject to availability:

_____	Volume I (1986-87)	$22.50
_____	Volume II (1987-88)	$22.50
_____	Volume III (1988-89)	$22.50
_____	Volume IV (1989-90)	$22.50
_____	Volume V (1990-91)	$22.50
_____	Volume VI (1991-92)	$25.00
_____	Limited offer: Volumes VII & VIII (1992-93 & 1993-94) $45.00	

_____ _____

(Note: Prices may change without notice. For current prices, phone (209) 255-4094 weekdays during office hours-Pacific time.)

Check your method of payment:

☐ Check enclosed in the amount of _____
☐ Purchase order attached (Please be sure it includes the P.O. number, the authorizing signature, and the position of the authorizing person.)
☐ Visa or MasterCard # _____
   (circle one)

Expires_____

Signature_____

Make checks payable to **AIMS Education Foundation.**
Mail to **AIMS Newsletter, P.O. Box 8120, Fresno, CA 93747-8120.**

AIMS Duplication Rights Program

AIMS has received many requests from school districts for the purchase of unlimited duplication rights to *AIMS* materials. In response, the *AIMS Education Foundation* has formulated the program outlined below. There is a built-in flexibility which, we trust, will provide for those who use *AIMS* materials extensively to purchase such rights for either individual activities or entire books.

It is the goal of the *AIMS Education Foundation* to make its materials and programs available at reasonable cost. All income from sale of publications and duplication rights is used to support *AIMS* programs. Hence, strict adherence to regulations governing duplication is essential. Duplication of *AIMS* materials beyond limits set by copyright laws and those specified below is strictly forbidden.

Limited Duplication Rights

Any purchaser of an AIMS book may make up to *200 copies* of any activity in that book for use at *one school site*. Beyond that, rights must be purchased according to the appropriate category.

Unlimited Duplication Rights for Single Activities

An individual or school may purchase the right to make an unlimited number of copies of a single activity. The royalty is $5.00 per activity per school site.

Examples: 3 activities x 1 site   x $5.00 = $15.00
9 activities x 3 sites x $5.00 = $135.00

Unlimited Duplication Rights for Whole Books

A school or district may purchase the right to make an unlimited number of copies of a single, *specified* book. The royalty is $20.00 per book per school site. This is in addition to the cost of the book.

Examples: 5 books   x 1 site   x $20.00 = $100.00
12 books x 10 sites x $20.00 = $2400.00

Newsletter Duplication Rights

Members of the *AIMS Education Foundation* who receive the *AIMS Newsletter* may make an unlimited number of copies of activities for use only at the member's school site. School districts must join separately for each school desiring to duplicate activities.

Workshop Instructors' Duplication Rights

Workshop instructors may distribute to registered workshop participants: a maximum of 100 copies of any article and /or 100 copies of no more than 8 activities, provided these 6 conditions are met:

1. Since all *AIMS* activities are based upon the *AIMS Model of Mathematics* and the *AIMS Model of Learning*, leaders must include in their presentations an explanation of these two models.
2. Workshop instructors must relate the *AIMS* activities presented to these basic explanations of the *AIMS* philosophy of education.
3. The copyright notice must appear on all materials distributed.
4. Instructors must provide information enabling participants to apply for membership in the *AIMS Education Foundation* or order books from the Foundation.
5. Instructors must inform participants of their limited duplication rights as outlined below.
6. Only student pages may be duplicated.

Written permission must be obtained for duplication beyond the limits listed above. Additional royalty payments may be required.

Workshop Participants' Rights

Those enrolled in workshops in which AIMS student activity sheets are distributed may duplicate a maximum of 35 copies or enough to use the lessons one time with one class, whichever is less. Beyond that, rights must be purchased according to the appropriate category.

Application for Duplication Rights

The purchasing agency or individual must clearly specify the following:
      1. Name, address, and telephone number
      2. Titles of the books for Unlimited Duplication Rights contracts
      3. Titles of activities for Unlimited Duplication Rights contracts
      4. Names and addresses of school sites for which duplication rights are being purchased

NOTE: Books to be duplicated must be purchased separately and are not included in the contract for Unlimited Duplication Rights.

The requested duplication rights are automatically authorized when proper payment is received, although a *Certificate of Duplication Rights* will be issued when the application is processed.

Address all correspondence to
      Contract Division
      AIMS Education Foundation
      P.O. Box 8120
      Fresno, CA 93747-8120